AF085065

Landscapes of
JERSEY

a countryside guide
Seventh edition

Geoff Daniel
updated by Sunflower Books

SUNFLOWER BOOKS

For Rik, with love

Seventh edition
Copyright © 2024
Sunflower Books™
PO Box 36160
London SW7 3WS, UK
www.sunflowerbooks.co.uk

All rights reserved.
No part of this publication
may be reproduced, stored
in a retrieval system, or
transmitted by any form
or by any means,
electronic, mechanical,
photocopying, recording
or otherwise, without the
prior written permission
of the publishers.
Sunflower Books and
'Landscapes' are
Registered Trademarks.

ISBN 978-1-85691-559-5

Rozel woods (Walk 9 and Picnic 9)

Important note to the reader

We have tried to ensure that the descriptions and maps in this book are error-free at press date. The book is updated, where necessary, whenever future printings are undertaken. It will be very helpful for us to receive your comments (sent to info@sunflowerbooks.co.uk, please) for the updating of future editions.

We also rely on those who use this book — especially walkers — to use their common sense as well. Natural hazards are few in Jersey, but use good judgement when walking on cliff-tops in windy conditions, and allow plenty of time when exploring sea caves or beaches at low tide. The rising tide flows very quickly and can trap the unwary. Jersey does *not* have an extensive public footpath network: some tracks may look public, but are in fact on private land. We believe that all the walks in this book are on public roads, tracks and paths, but if you discover otherwise, please respect the wishes of the landowner. Abiding by the country code (page 23) is wise in any event.

Cover photograph: pink sea thrift at Le Pulec

Photographs by the author, with the exception of pages 1, 14, 16 (both), 20 (both) and cover: Shutterstock; 2, 10, 11, 19 (bottom two), 39, 40, 44, 49, 50, 51, 55 and 59: John Seccombe; 57: Jersey War Tunnels
Maps: Nick Hill for Sunflower Books. Base map data © OpenStreetMap contributors. Contour data made available under ODbL (opendatacommons.org/licenses/odbl/1.0)
A CIP catalogue record for this book is available from the British Library
Printed and bound in England: Short Run Press, Exeter

Contents

Preface	4
Getting about	7
Picnics and short walks	9
Touring	12
THE WAY WEST	14

St Helier • St Aubin • Noirmont • La Corbière • L'Etacq • Grosnez • La Grève de Lecq • Devil's Hole • Lion Park • Jersey War Tunnels (German Underground Military Hospital) • St Lawrence • Millbrook • St Helier

THE EAST END	18

St Helier • Sion • Pallot Steam Museum • (Bouley Bay) • Jersey's zoo • Rozel • St Catherine's Bay • Mont Orgueil • La Hougue Bie • La Rocque • Green Island • St Helier

Walking	22
Where to stay	22
Weather	22
What to take	23
A country code for walkers and motorists	23
Waymarking and maps	24

THE WALKS (● grading symbols are explained on page 24)
The walks (all circular except 7 and 11) are arranged starting with coastal walks running clockwise round the island from St Helier, followed by four inland walks. The symbol ➡ indicates short circular walks which are especially suitable for motorists.

●	1 St Helier heritage ➡	25
●	2 L'Ouaisné • St Brelade • Beauport • La Lande du L'Ouest • Corbière • ➡	29
●	3 Noirmont and Portelet Bay ➡	32
●	4 The Corbière walk	35
●	5 Le Val de la Mare (Short walk ➡)	37
●	6 The Pinnacle ➡	40
●	7 The north coast	42
●	8 Sorel and La Vallée des Mouriers ➡	45
●	9 Round St Martin's and Rozel	46
●	10 A short stroll around Flicquet ➡	50
●	11 St Catherine's to Gorey	52
●	12 St Lawrence: the heart of Jersey	53
●	13 Jersey War Tunnels (German Underground Hospital)	56
●	14 Gorey village and Queen's Valley (Short walk) ➡	58
●	15 La Hougue Bie (Short walk ➡)	60

Buses and inter-island transport	62
St Helier town plan	25
Index	64
Island touring map	*inside back cover*

 Preface

When you invest a little of your time and curiosity in Jersey, it feels much larger than only 45 square miles.

For the walker, Jersey expands with every step, for there is so much visual enjoyment and so much history to stir the imagination. Each bay, each stretch of cliff-top has a story to tell ... and each mile of country lane whispers secrets of its own.

To the motorist, a distance on paper means very little when translated to miles or kilometres per hour on this island, for whichever route is planned, there will be many a reason to stop and enjoy scenery, watering hole, or man-made attraction.

The picnicker is spoiled for choice of sites, whether opting for an official site with barbecue facilities or simply settling for a quiet spot along a walk route.

Landscapes of Jersey has been written for countryside enthusiasts. You will not find details of restaurants, hotels, shop opening hours, or other conventional guide book information here: these subjects are amply covered in a free guide given to all visitors when they arrive at the port or airport (or you can log on to the official website: www.jersey.com, in advance). Instead, I've concentrated on giving clear instructions for the car tours and walks, with some of my personal observations that may add interest to your exploration.

Whether you are a walker, a motorist, or simply taking a family holiday, you are assured of a warm Jersey welcome and if not a guarantee, then at least a fair chance of good weather. The Gulf Stream washes all the Channel Islands, and Jersey in particular has an excellent sunshine record, well above the UK average. Jersey's climate has been compared with that of southern Cornwall but drier and warmer. Even in winter, frosts are rare and snow even rarer. No matter what season it is, photographers will appreciate the quality of light in Jersey on any clear day.

Jersey's past
Invasion in one form or another has been a key factor in Jersey's history for a thousand years.

In the 9th century Viking raiders plundered all the Channel Islands, regarding them as a bonus on pillaging

Here is a Chusan palm (Trachycarpus fortunei) seen during Walk 4 to Corbière. Palm trees come as no surprise: Jersey's climate has been compared with that of southern Cornwall, but even warmer.

voyages to Britain and France.

Between the 13th and 15th centuries, France repeatedly tried to regain control of what was once theirs, for the islands were (and still are) part of the Duchy of Normandy. The then Duke of Normandy, King John, relinquished the mainland duchy to France in 1204, so the Channel Islands are, in fact, all that remain of the Duchy of Normandy; King Charles is the Duke of Normandy (one of his oldest titles).

In the Napoleonic era, France sided with the American colonists in their fight for independence and thus declared war on Britain. This resulted in defensive towers going up around Jersey (some are Martello towers, others are more accurately described as 'Jersey round towers', but they are similar in appearance).

Most recently, Jersey was occupied for five years during World War II by Nazi forces (see the Noirmont walk on page 32 and Jersey War Tunnels on page 56). But oddly, though concrete bunkers and towers proliferate, they seem to add a dimension to the landscape, rather than ruin it.

Jersey's present

The island's independent government of elected representatives is known as *Les Etats* — the States of Jersey. This refers to the three estates — the Court, the Church and the People. The President and Speaker is the Bailiff, appointed by the Crown. The *Vicomte* (sheriff) carries the Royal Mace (the gift of King Charles II), the symbol of the Bailiff's authority. The Bailiff is also the President and Chief Judge of the Royal Court, where he is assisted by *Jurats* (honourary magistrates). Law officers are appointed by the Crown; they may speak but not vote. The Lieutenant Governor represents the King; he may attend, but takes no part in debates.

Much of what you see will be familiar to British visitors. Indeed, many Britons have settled in Jersey (not easy now, because of strict residential qualifications). However, scores of roads and streets have French names, while the Jersey accent derives from a time when the Jersey-Norman patois was more widely used than it is now. It is plain fact that for all Jersey's historical antipathy to France, the French mainland is easily visible on most days ... a mere 17 miles away.

Jersey's reputation as a financial centre is well known: some 50 major banks and finance houses are based on the island. Income tax is low (20%), corporation tax even lower (0%!), and while UK VAT does not apply, a local general sales tax (GST; currently 5%) is added to the price of goods. Some shopkeepers absorb or waive the GST, particularly when charging the full UK price (including VAT), citing transport costs to make up the difference. But other shopkeepers deduct VAT, so look for competitive pricing. You can use UK currency on the island, but you'll often receive change in Jersey notes (£1, £5 or £10) or coins. Jersey notes can be exchanged free of commission at any UK bank.

Acknowledgements

I am indebted to the following for help in preparing the original and subsequent editions of this book:

The States of Jersey Island Development Committee;
Howard B Baker of St Helier, whose intimate knowledge of Jersey, warmly shared, was of immense value, and whose own reference map 'The German Occupation of Jersey 1940/45' was a thorough and revealing document on the island's wartime experience;
Jersey Tourism, for information, hospitality and mobility;
Mike Freeman, States of Jersey Conservation Department, for information on Jersey's natural history;
The Jersey Society (La Société Jersiaise) for use of its library;
Channel Islands Occupation Society;
Sue Hardy, who checked several editions and who devised Walk 12;
John Seccombe and the Sunflower Books team for constant updating.

Books

Landscapes of Jersey is primarily a guide to countryside exploration and is intended to be used in tandem with a standard guide. Many more locally-published books on specific subjects such as bird watching or the Occupation years (or indeed, other walking guides) may be found in St Helier bookshops and many island newsagents and gift shops.

Also of interest

Landscapes of Guernsey (with Alderney, Sark and Herm), a companion book to this one, also published by Sunflower Books

Getting about

A **hired car** is the most practical way of exploring Jersey, though by no means the only way. There is a wide choice of makes and models, and most vehicles are brand new. Hire vehicles are distinguished on the island by the prefix letter 'H' on the car's number plate. You can also take your own car, but a caravan or camper van may only be driven from ferry to campsite at a prebooked time, and there are size restrictions.

To be able to hire a car, visitors must provide a valid driving licence with no endorsements for dangerous driving or drink/driving within the past five years. (Holders of photocard licences must also have the paper form D470 with them; *see important reference to this on page 12*.) Drivers must be over 20 years of age, but there is no upper age limit (subject to any hire car insurance company proviso). Collision damage waiver is not compulsory but, if you do not take this option, you may be asked for a hefty deposit to cover part of the insurance excess (sometimes £500 or more), and this amount would become your responsibility in the event of damage to the car. It's up to you whether you pay the extra for CDW and peace of mind. Do shop around for car hire: some firms allow a useful discount provided you book with them direct rather than through an agent or a hotel.

Motor cycles, **mopeds** and **scooters** can also be hired; the wearing of crash helmets by rider and pillion passenger is compulsory.

Petrol carries slightly less duty than in the UK and is therefore marginally cheaper. On the fold-out touring map and in the touring notes, I have not attempted to list the location of every filling station, because there are so many; it would be difficult to drive five miles without seeing one! (Likewise, although the touring map indicates the locations of some cafés, restaurants and attractions, it is by no means comprehensive in this respect, and you will come across many more.)

Parking places and official car parks are plentiful; many are free of charge (most parking is free of charge between 5pm and 8am). At paying parks, you cannot pay cash but must display scratch paycards, on which you indicate date and time of arrival. These are sold by garages and many shops. Even at the height of the season, it's not difficult to find parking space, except perhaps in the main car parks in St Helier (or areas set aside for residents' parking). However, it is usually easy to find a space in the huge Pier Road multi-storey park, only five or six minutes' walk from St Helier centre. There are a few limited-waiting parking places in St Helier, some needing a paycard, others permitting free parking with a parking disc. The latter is sometimes provided with a hire car. If not, you can purchase one at the Town Hall, Motor Traffic Office, or at post offices. (If you do not have a parking disc, it is permissible to use a paycard instead in any parking disc area.) But you'll find free parks all over the island where you'll need neither disc nor paycard.

There is an all-island **maximum speed restriction** of 40mph/64kph, but in many places the limit is less than this, sometimes as low as 15mph/24kph. Places and junctions where you must halt are indicated by a yellow line across the road. A single yellow line parallel with the kerb or pavement means no waiting at all (the equivalent of a double yellow line in the UK). There are many roundabouts with a 'filter in turn' system — watch out for the signs. At these, one vehicle at a time enters the roundabout from each road joining it, everyone taking their 'turn'. It can be a bit confusing when you are not used to it, but it works!

The **legal limit for alcohol** consumption is the same as in England: 80 mg of alcohol per 100 ml of blood).

Some country roads are designated '**green lanes**' with a 15mph speed limit for safer walking and cycling. Special road signs alert motorists using these routes.

Buses operate throughout the island from a central bus and coach station at Liberation Square, St Helier. There's a very frequent service to popular centres such as St Aubin and Gorey, but the service to more distant points is also good, and especially useful for walkers doing sections of the north coast path. See pages 62-63.

Cyclists are catered for by several cycle hire depots, and bicycles can be hired for a day or by the week.

Taxi ranks can be found at the airport and in St Helier, and there are numerous private hire companies operating. There are set tariffs, with fares clearly shown on a meter, and with different tariffs applying to day and night hire, and on public holidays.

Island excursions are run by Jersey Bus & Coach Tours, Tantivy Blue Coaches and Waverley Coaches. Excursions to the **other Channel Islands** or day trips to **France** can be made by sea or air; see page 63.

Picnics and short walks

Picnicking is a particular pleasure in Jersey, where there are so many suitable settings. I have chosen some of my favourites; many are accessible by bus, as well as by car or bicycle. Jersey can be breezy — check the wind direction before choosing your picnic place!

All the information you need to get to these picnic spots is given below, where *picnic numbers correspond to walk numbers*. Beside the picnic title you'll find a map reference: the exact location of the picnic spot is shown on this *walking map* with the symbol P. I also include transport details (🚌 = how to get there by bus; 🚗 = where to park), how long a walk you will have, and any other information you might find useful. Some picnic sites have tables (and sometimes barbecues); these are indicated by a ⊓ in the list below and on the touring map.

Ready-prepared picnic fare can be obtained at Marks & Spencers in St Helier, but *do* patronise the local shops as well: try the take-aways at one of the numerous outlets in St Helier — around the market and along The Esplanade near the bus station.

Please remember that if more than a few minutes' walking is required, you will need to wear **sensible shoes** and to take a **sunhat** (○ indicates a picnic in full sun). A stout groundsheet also comes in handy, in case the ground is damp or prickly.

1 ELIZABETH CASTLE (touring map and St Helier plan on page 25; photo on page 28) ○

🚌 by bus: 30min on foot. Bus to St Helier
🚗 by car: up to 30min on foot. Park in St Helier (paycard required).
Reached on foot by causeway at low tide from opposite the Grand Hotel (or you can ride across in one of the amphibious vehicles). *Picnic in the castle grounds (where there are plenty of benches). Allow 2 hours if you decide to visit the museums (admission charge).*

2 BEAUPORT (map on page 30; photo on page 11) ○

🚌 by bus: 20-30min on foot. Bus 12 or 12a to St Brelade's Bay. From St Brelade's Church (see map) take the signposted footpath to the bay.
🚗 by car: Park at the free car park above Beauport Bay, reached on narrow roads signposted from St Brelade's Church or by the first left turn just after turning onto the B83 road to Corbière. (Picnic spots near the car park; or allow 10-20min to get down to the beach.)
A beautiful, unspoiled little bay, really gorgeous on a warm, clear evening. Sit on grassy banks or sand.

The extensive dunes of Les Mielles: a maze of paths with many picnic places, both official and impromptu (Picnic 5a; near Walk 5)

3 NOIRMONT (map on page 33; photos on pages 15 and 34) ○ 🍴

🚌 by bus: 10min on foot. Bus 12a to Portelet. From the terminus take the cliff-top path in the corner of the car park overlooking the bay. This will lead you through gorse and heather to Noirmont Point.
🚗 by car: under 5min on foot. Park at Noirmont (ample free parking).
Dazzling views of the coastline and St Helier from this striking headland. .

4 LA CORBIÈRE (map on page 30; photos on page 16 and 36) ○

🚌 by bus: up to 15min on foot. Bus 12, 12a or 22 to La Corbière
🚗 by car: up to 15min on foot. Park at La Corbière (free).
Stunning views from this exposed southwest corner; enjoy a stroll to the lighthouse. Some benches at viewpoints, nice grassy spots.

5a LA MIELLE DE MORVILLE (touring map; photo above) 🍴

🚌 by bus: up to 15min on foot. Bus 22 or X22 to Five Mile Avenue and walk south 200 yards/metres to the road to Jersey National Park
🚗 by car: up to 5min on foot. Park at the Jersey National Park, just off the road behind St Ouen's Bay (free).
Organised sites with barbecues, or scores of places in the dunes. There are information boards about nature trails and bird hides overlooking the pools of water.

5b LE VAL DE LA MARE (map on page 37; photo on page 38)

🚌 by bus: 30min on foot. Bus 9 to Val de la Mare car park
🚗 by car: 30min on foot. Free parking at Val de la Mare on the A12.
Follow Walk 5 (page 37) for 15min, but turn *right*, to skirt the western arm of the reservoir for a further 15min.
Grassy slopes and convenient benches; splendid views over St Ouen's Bay. Shade from trees nearby.

6 THE PINNACLE (map on reverse of touring map; photo on page 41) ○

🚌 by bus: up to 20min on foot. Bus Bus 22 or X22 to L'Etacq (terminus)
🚗 by car: up to 20min on foot. Park at Le Poulec or L'Etacq (free).
Follow Walk 6 (page 40) from the bus terminus; some steep gradients.
Magnificent (but isolated) cliff-top setting. Do not climb down the slopes, as cliff erosion has made this hazardous. Stout shoes essential.

The delightful little bay of Beauport (Car tour 2, Walk 2 and Picnic 2)

7 BOULEY BAY (map on reverse of touring map) ○

🚌 by bus: up to 30min on foot. Bus 4 to Trinity Church, then take the (signposted) road to Bouley Bay.
🚗 by car: up to 20min on foot. Park (free) on the jetty just to the west of the bay (access via the narrow C96, north of Trinity Church, and the C102).
Picnic on the beach. Otherwise walk up the fairly steep track to Le Jardin d'Olivet, the scene of a battle in 1549.

9 ROZEL WOODS (map page 47; photos on pages 2 and 19)

🚗 by car: 10min on foot. See page 46 for free parking details.
Follow Walk 9 (page 46) into the woods, past the small pond.
Benches available; good shade.

11a ARCHIRONDEL (map on page 47) ⛱

🚗 by car: up to 10min on foot. Park at Archirondel Tower (free).
Two barbecue areas lie off the B29 north of the tower. Shade nearby.

11b ANNE PORT (map on page 47) ⛱ ○

🚗 by car: no walking. Park at the site (B29, north of Mont Orgueil).
Fine views from this headland at the north end of the bay. Tables, but no barbecues.

12 WATERWORKS VALLEY (map on page 54)

🚗 by car: no walking. Two picnic spots (free parking) on the C119
Tree-lined countryside near the reservoirs. Benches, but no tables.

14 QUEEN'S VALLEY RESERVOIR (map page 47; photo on page 59)

🚌 by bus: 15min on foot. Bus 13 to St Saviour's Hospital
🚗 by car: 15min on foot. Park at the St Saviour's Hospital end of the Queen's Valley Reservoir (free).
Follow the path along the eastern bank of the lake, until you reach the causeway. Pass it and, under 5min later, climb a couple of steps to a grassy bank with pleasant views over the lake. Shade nearby.

15 LA HOUGUE BIE (map on page 60, photo on page 20) ⛱

🚌 by bus: no walking. Bus 13 to La Hougue Bie
🚗 by car: no walking. Park at La Hougue Bie (free).
No barbecues, but much to see: large underground neolithic/megalithic chamber, medieval chapels, geological and archaeological exhibits, wartime memorial in an underground bunker. Drinks available; ample shade.

Touring

Jersey is an island roughly nine miles by five (15km by 8km), with about 450 miles of good, if sometimes narrow roads. Exploring this road network will take more time than you might imagine: not only is there is much to see and do en route, but there is an **island-wide speed limit of 40mph/ 64kmph** (even less in some places). And rightly so. This is not an island to be taken in a hurry. However you put together your day, it would be difficult not to enjoy it in Jersey.

Most visitors like to hire a car for their stay on the island. You can take your own car if you wish, by conventional car ferry from Portsmouth or by high speed catamaran from Poole in Dorset. Drink-driving and seat-belt laws are similar to those in the rest of Britain and are keenly enforced. Visiting drivers **must** carry their licence, including the paper form D470 containing information on penalty points/ driving convictions. Since the DVLC has withdrawn these, it's a good idea to know how to obtain an 'access code' if you intend to hire a car. The code will allow the car hire company to inspect this information online on the DVLC website. You can get your personal code from the DVLC website by entering your driving licence and National Insurance numbers. But note that the code is only valid for 21 days.

For further information on car hire and driving on the island, see page 7.

The touring notes are brief: they include little information available in standard guides. Instead, I concentrate on taking you to my favourite natural and man-made attractions, and I emphasise possibilities for **picnicking** and **walking**, with a good selection of circular walks for motorists (see Contents, page 3). Some walk and picnic numbers are shown in parentheses in the tour headings: they are nearby, but you must take a *detour* to reach them.

The pull-out touring map is designed to be held out opposite the touring notes. This map deliberately omits many of the lesser roads, but all the roads I would recommend for car touring are included, and you may find it easier to use while motoring than some of the free give-away maps that are available at the port or airport. When motoring near a walk (indicated by large green numbers), you may wish to use the touring map in tandem with the 1:25,000 walking maps printed in the book.

It is important to note that you can do a circuit quite easily and take your choice of north-south routes along several picturesque valleys. Moreover, by creating a circuit using coast road and one of the central valleys, you will see the best of Jersey. *But beware: east-west tours across the middle of the island are a different matter: signposting is 'discreet' — or non-existent! It is very easy to lose your sense of direction and find yourself driving round in circles! Unless you know the lanes intimately, you are almost certain to get lost.*

I offer two main route suggestions with optional side-tracks to take in some of the more popular attractions. Please remember that changes can take place at very short notice — businesses change hands; authorities may change opening hours or restrict access. So, if there's something that you would particularly like to see, do check with the Jersey Tourism office, or telephone the attraction you plan to visit, before making a special journey.

Cumulative distances are given from St Helier (see town plan, page 25). A **key to the symbols** in the notes is on the touring map.

The gorgeous sweep of Gorey Harbour, seen from Mont Orgueil castle (Car tour 2, Walk 11)

Car tour 1: THE WAY WEST

St Helier • St Aubin • Noirmont • La Corbière • L'Etacq • Grosnez • La Grève de Lecq • Devil's Hole • Jersey War Tunnels (German Underground Military Hospital) • St Lawrence • Millbrook • St Helier

37mi/60km; about 2-3 hours' driving plus time for visits en route

On route: 🅿 at Noirmont, La Mielle de Morville, L'Etacq; Picnics (see pages 9-11): (2), 3, 4, 5a, (5b), 6, (7), 12; Walks (2), 3, 4, (5), 6, 7, (8), 12, 13

All roads on this route are in excellent condition, but be prepared for a few hairpin bends and some very narrow lanes. Watch your speed!

From St Helier, head out on the Esplanade following signs to 'ST BRELADE, THE WEST' (A2). When the dual carriageway ends after about two miles, keep left, joining the A1 for 'BEAUMONT, ST AUBIN'; then, at a Y-fork in **Beaumont**, keep left to **St Aubin**★ (3.5mi ♦▲▲✕🅿🚉WC). This is a quieter resort area than St Helier, with a delightful harbour. Keep to the narrow harbour road as you leave St Aubin, then turn right uphill just past The Old Court House Inn hotel. It's a very narrow road here, through a series of hairpin bends and then alongside the walled grounds of a country house on your left. Give way as you join the B57 ('Noirmont Road'), where you turn left and then keep straight ahead to the memorial headland of **Noirmont**★ (6mi 📷🅿*P*3), shown opposite and described on page 33.

Return on the B57, passing roads on your left to Portelet Common (Alternative walk 2, with a splendid view over the bay) and L'Ouaisné (🚉✕WC), where Walk 2 begins. Join the A13 and turn left. Stay on the main road only briefly until, at a fork, you drop down left on the B66 to **St Brelade's Bay**★ (8mi ♦▲▲✕⊕🚉WC). There are several adventure sports companies (kayaking, paddleboarding, etc) at this superb beach. St Brelade's lovely church is at the end of the road, just above the harbour; take time to visit the graveyard and the Fishermen's Chapel as well. Then, from the entrance/lych gate, turn right for 'BEAUPORT BAY'. Climb through more hairpin bends and pass the road to Beauport★ (■📷🅿*P*2; photograph page 11) on your left: perhaps make a detour to look at this very pretty, unspoiled cove.

Otherwise, come to a T-junction and turn left on the B83 to **La Corbière**★ (10mi 📷▲▲✕🅿WC*P*4; Walk 4), one of the best-known sights in Jersey, and really spectacular if you catch it at sunset or when the sea is running high over the rocks in a sou'west gale! Continue on the B44, then turn left on the B35. You pass a signposted path to La Sergenté, the oldest tomb on the island (12mi ⛨; Walk 4), with parking nearby. Now you're at the southern end of **St Ouen's Bay**, a glorious five-mile sweep of beach, much favoured by

Walk 3 and Picnic 3: World War II weaponry at Noirmont, the headland memorial to Jersey's war dead. St Helier is in the distance. See also the photo on page 34. Below: Devil's Hole

surfers. Continue north past **Les Mielles Nature Reserve** on the right and the **Kempt Tower** on the left — a true Martello Tower, built in 1834 and named for one of Wellington's generals at Waterloo. There are picnic sites and bird hides in **La Mielle de Morville** (*P*5a) opposite, and occasional guided walks in the nature reserve: details from Jersey Tourism (01534 859000) or the National Trust for Jersey (01534 483193).

The unusual boat-shaped building on the sea wall is let out for self-catering holidays by Jersey Heritage. Near the Château Plaisir shopping complex (including Jersey Woollen

Above: the ruined 14th-century castle at Grosnez (Walks 6 and 7); left: La Corbière

Mills) is the **Channel Islands Military Museum**, housing German and Allied vehicles and memorabilia in a former Nazi bunker (**M🖃**). Opposite is **Jersey Pearl**, a spacious emporium and restaurant.

At the end of this long, straight stretch of road, turn right. After about 700 yards/metres, turn sharp left on the B35. This low-lying area is **L'Etacq★**, which terminates in the imposing rock formation of Le Grand Etacquerel (17.5mi 📷). Walk 6 starts here with a steep climb to the heathland of Les Landes and visits the magnificent rock pinnacle shown on page 41 (*P*6). Climb the hill, then make a very sharp left turn at the top, on the B55 to **Grosnez★** (19mi ■📷), where Walk 7 starts and Walk 6 can also start. Head off on the track to the ruined 14th-century castle and enjoy the magnificent views (information boards describe its history). There is ample free parking.

Return to the B55

and head left, then go left again to **Plémont**★ (∩🅿︎🍴WC; Walk 7), where there is an excellent beach, a good beach café and caves to explore at low tide though parking (free) is very limited.

Return again to the B55 and turn left. After a little over a mile, turn sharp left on the B65 to **La Grève de Lecq**★ (22mi ⛰︎✕ 🍴🅿︎🚍MWC — plenty of free parking space here.) There's another fine beach and a 19th-century barracks owned by the National Trust for Jersey. This is worth a visit: there's an impressive collection of horse-drawn vehicles, an exhibition revealing the story of Grève de Lecq's past and its tourist attractions, a special exhibition devoted to Jersey's north coast, a gift shop and visitor centre and, of course, exhibits devoted to its military history. Walk 7 passes here, too.

Head out of La Grève de Lecq on the B40, then turn left on the B33 and left again on the C103. Pass La Mare Wine Estate and come to **Devil's Hole**★ (25mi ∩🅿︎🍴WC), where a steepish path leads from the parking area (free) down to a wild sea inlet and the impressive blowhole shown on page 15.

Continue south on the B26, heading down the valley and bearing left on the A11 at a fork. At the T-junction by the Victoria pub and hotel (on the left) turn right towards the 'JERSEY WAR TUNNELS'. Some 300 yards past the hotel, there is a small car park on the right, near a mill pond. Stop here briefly and walk through a lovely bit of woodland to **Le Moulin de Quetivel**, a mill of 14th-century origin (en route in Walk 13).

Signposting now takes you left on the B89 and left again to the to the **Jersey War Tunnels**★ (32mi M🚍WC). Walk 13 (page 56) starts and ends here.

After your visit, from the Tunnels car park cross straight over onto Rue de La Ville Emphrie, instead of bearing right into Meadow Bank (the way you came). Turn left on the A10 at **La Ville Emphrie** and go through **St Lawrence** (34mi; Walk 12). Under 300 yards/metres beyond the church, at a Y-fork, bear right into La Rue des Corvees. Then take the second right turn into Rue de la Patente (C119). This becomes Chemin des Moulins and loops around to the right, to a T-junction. Turn right here on the C118, to go down **Waterworks Valley** (*P*12). This road winds delightfully between wooded slopes, reservoirs and meadows. You reach the A1 at **Millbrook**, where a left turn will take you back to **St Helier** (37mi).

Car tour 2: THE EAST END

St Helier • Sion • Pallot Steam Museum • (Bouley Bay) • Jersey's zoo • Rozel • St Catherine's Bay • Mont Orgueil • La Hougue Bie • La Rocque • Green Island • St Helier

24mi/38km; about 2 hours' driving plus time for visits en route

On route: ⌒ at St Catherine's Bay, La Hougue Bie; Picnics (see pages 9-11): (7b), 9, 11a, 11b, 14, 15; Walks 7, 9, 10, 11, 14, 15

All roads are excellent but narrow in places, with sharp bends (especially near Rozel. Stick to the 40mph speed limit.

From St Helier, head out on the Esplanade initially following signs to 'ST BRELADE, THE WEST' (A2), but get in the right-hand lane by the time you approach the end of the Esplanade, now following 'RING, ROAD, THE NORTH (A9)'. Go around the roundabout and take the exit for 'RING, ROAD, THE NORTH (B87)'. This road follows the curve of the park (which is on your left). Get into the right-hand lane and at the traffic lights turn right along Cheapside for 'RING ROAD, A9'. Follow the ring road left into Elizabeth Place and continue along Rouge Bouillon. Watch the signs and take the first exit from the roundabout at the Queen's Road junction; this is the A9.

You leave the town behind as you take the Grand Route de St Jean and come to **Sion** (3mi), where there is an old Methodist Chapel (✝ 1880) on the left built like a temple. It is enormous in relation to the size of the village. It closed for worship in 2010; the land has been sold, but the building will be protected. Past the chapel, on the right, is Macpela Cemetery, where European exiles who made Jersey their home in the mid-19th century were buried.

About a quarter of a mile past the chapel, turn right into Rue de Bechet, looking out for the signs to the fascinating **Pallot Steam Museum★** (M). This is an extensive, if informal collection assembled over several years by a local engineer, Mr Pallot. There are steam and diesel railway engines, rolling stock and a few hundred yards of full standard gauge railway track laid out in a circuit in the field behind the museum where, if you choose the right time to visit, you can ride in a train like the one shown opposite. In any case, at least one item is operating under steam at all times the museum is open. There are traction engines, rare old farm machines and other machines of all kinds ... there's even an organ room! Truly a surprising sight, tucked away in the heart of the island.

Leave the museum on a minor road opposite the entrance, to join the B51, where you turn right. From Trinity Church (5mi) you could make a short detour (about 4mi return)

One of the gorillas from the famous colony at Jersey's zoo

down to **Bouley Bay**★ (⛺📷✖🍴WC*P*7b): turn left just past the church and then turn sharp right when you reach the C96. Follow the zigzag road (sometimes used for hill-climb motor racing) down to the bay, which is on the north coast path (Walk 7).

The main drive continues straight ahead from Trinity Church, on the B31. At 6mi come to the famous Durrell Wildlife Conservation Trust (**Jersey's zoo**★), which does splendid work in breeding rare species and is noted for its gorilla colony. This is a must, though it's probably best to reserve at least half a day for your visit here as admission is quite expensive and there is much to see.

After passing the zoo entrance (on the right), turn left on the C93 signposted to 'ROZEL'. Now a pleasant run above the coastal path takes you along to **Rozel**★ (9mi ⛺✖

Right: a 1931 steam locomotive hauling Victorian coaches on the full-size standard gauge railway at the Pallot Steam Museum.
Below: this pleasant spot near the entrance to Rozel woods (Picnic 9 and Walk 9) is only a few minutes' walk from a convenient parking spot at La Maison slipway.

📷 ♿WC), where Walk 7 ends. It's an attractive little fishing village with a hotel, restaurant, pub and café — possibly ideal for an away-from-it-all holiday. To join circular Walk 9 here at Rozel, see the map on page 47 and notes on page 48.

Climb out of Rozel on the B38 and look out for the B91 on the left, signed to 'FLICQUET'. Reach a minor crossroads (on the route of both Walk 9 and Walk 10) and turn right for 'ST CATHERINE'S', soon passing riding stables. Beyond the hamlets of Les Mares and Le Villot, you join the B29 for 'ST CATHERINE'S'. Turn left. You pass a car park at La Mare slipway, where Walk 9

This medieval chapel rises above the burial chamber at La Hougue Bie (Walk and Picnic 15); below: Dolmen de Faldouët (Walk 11)

Car tour 2: The east end

begins (*P*9). Then come to **St Catherine's Bay**★ and Breakwater (12mi ⚐🎦⬛WC), where Walks 10 and 11 begin. There is plenty of free parking here, so why not stretch your legs on the breakwater or try the short Walk 10 circuit?

From St Catherine's Bay return on the B29, first coming to **Archirondel** (⬛*P*11a with ⚐) and then **Anne Port** (WC*P*11b with ⚐). Coming to a T-junction, take a sharp left to head down into **Gorey** (14mi ⛪🏠🏨✕🚻⊕⬛WC) and park by the harbour. Walk up to **Mont Orgueil Castle**★ (🏛🎦); the magnificent view from here is shown on pages 12-13. Walk 11 (from St Catherine's) ends here. From either Anne Port or Gorey you could make an interesting diversion (signposted) to the **Dolmen de Faldouët** (⊓) shown opposite. See Walk 11 and the map on page 47.

From Gorey harbour head back the way you came in initially, but then keep straight ahead on the B28 *(not signed when last seen)*. Watch for a sign, 'HOUGUE BIE' half a mile along, and turn left. Then turn left again after just 100 yards (still the B28, still *not signed*). Short walk 14 starts at St Saviour's Hospital (15mi), at the northern end of the **Queen's Valley Reservoir** (*P*14, photo on page 59). Continue to **La Hougue Bie**★ (16mi ⛪⊓M⚐*P*15), where the chapel shown opposite is just off to your left. Walk 15 begins here (details on page 60).

Leaving La Hougue Bie, head back the way you came. After 350 yards turn right on the B37, passing La Hougue Grange on your left. The road bends 90° left. Follow it to a T-junction, where you bear right until you come to the A3. At this point you *could* return to St Helier by turning right and taking an inland route via Georgetown.

But the main tour turns left towards 'GROUVILLE CHURCH/GOREY'. Past **Grouville** you reach the A4, where you turn right. This gives you a chance to look at more of the coast. The seaward views are quite amazing at low tide, when the sea can recede more than two miles, revealing treacherous reefs. Your return to St Helier will be via **La Rocque**, **Le Hocq**, and **Le Croc** (honest: look at the map!), each of which has some parking space, permitting a break of journey for a brief look round.

As you near St Helier, you have a choice of routes, either via the road tunnel (turn right when you see the appropriate signs) or staying on the coast road past the open-air pool at Havre des Pas, eventually turning right into Pier Road. You pass the **Jersey Museum**★ (**M**) on the left, before turning left to arrive back at Liberation Square and the Maritime Museum (24mi).

Walking

The walks in this book are designed to take you to the loveliest parts of Jersey on the best footpaths.

Beginners: You can do most of the walks without problems, but the less nimble might find some stretches of the north coast path too steep for their liking.

Experienced walkers: All walks should be within your capability, including the north coast. This could be achieved in a day, but I would recommend making at least two days of it, to enjoy its sights fully.

All walkers: Please follow routes as described in the notes, especially where they are off-road. If at any stage you are uncertain of the way forward, go back to your last 'sure' point and start again. Do *not* try to continue a walk which for some reason has become impassable. And *I cannot emphasise too strongly* the need for caution when exploring Jersey's beaches at low tide. *Be absolutely sure of the tide times (check the local paper, or buy the tide tables at a shop) and always allow plenty of time to reach a safe point.*

Where to stay

Except perhaps during July and August, accommodation should never pose a problem: Jersey has an excellent range of registered hotels and guest houses (inspected and graded annually by Jersey Tourism). The Tourism website (www.jersey.com) has ample details of accommodation. Self-catering accommodation is harder to come by, so it is best to book early in the year.

While most people stay around **St Helier**, you may prefer **St Aubin** or **St Brelade's Bay** to the west or **Gorey** in the east. Both are charming centres, with good public transport links to St Helier. There are also some pleasant small hotels and guest houses along the north coast and deep inland in the countryside.

Weather

Jersey has a summer average of 8 sunny hours a day (among the best in the British Isles); rainfall averages 33-39 inches (80-100 cm) a year. May to July are generally considered the best months to visit. August is warm, but can be thundery. March and April are often dry and sunny, and Jersey has known many an autumn 'Indian summer'.

What to take

For much of the country walking in this book, you will need little special equipment. Some walkers find trainers adequate, but I always recommend lightweight boots which cope with almost any conditions underfoot, which in Jersey might include long wet grass, rock pools, sand dunes, muddy tracks and tarmac roads … all on the same walk! Below is a checklist of items you might find useful, depending on the season, the weather, and the part of the island covered by your walk:

- long-sleeved shirt and long trousers
- waterproof trousers and windcheat
- spare jumper, extra socks
- sunhat, suncream, sunglasses
- telephone numbers of taxi operators
- binoculars and camera
- small rucksack
- first aid kit
- bus timetable
- mobile/smartphone

A country code for walkers and motorists

The experienced rambler is used to following a 'country code', but the tourist who rarely ventures into the countryside may unwittingly cause damage or harm animals. Be aware of the following when walking:

- **Do not light fires** except at official barbecue sites. Never allow youngsters to play with matches, and never throw cigarette ends away. Fires are a very real hazard on headlands during dry summers and are difficult to deal with because of inaccessibility.
- **Keep dogs under proper control**, and **fasten all gates after you**.
- **Keep to paths** across farmland and avoid damage to fences, hedges and walls.
- **Leave no litter**: take it away or put it in a litter bin.
- **Protect wild and cultivated plants**, and never walk over cultivated land.
- **Go carefully** on narrow country roads, and don't block them by parking carelessly.
- **Respect the countryside** and the country way of life.
- The bird life of Jersey's coastal region is very important. **Do not disturb or annoy the birds**, especially during the nesting season (spring).

Below are some other points, particularly directed to walkers planning a lengthy ramble in any of the more remote locations:

- **Do not walk alone**, and *always* tell a responsible person where you are going and what time you expect to return. If you walk in a group, and someone is injured, others can seek help.

- **Do not overestimate your speed**; your pace will depend on the slowest walker in the group.
- **If a walk becomes unsafe**, do not press ahead.
- **Transport** at the end of a long walk is important.
- Carry some **warm clothing** and **extra rations**, even in summer, in case you are delayed beyond sunset.

Grading, waymarking, maps, GPS

The Contents on page 3 give you a quick overview of each walk's **grade**. Here are more details:

● very easy — more or less level (perhaps with a short climb to a viewpoint); good surfaces underfoot; easily followed

● easy-moderate — ascents/descents of no more than about 300-500m/ 1000-1800ft; good surfaces underfoot; easily followed

● moderate-strenuous — ascents/descents may be over 500m/1800ft; variable surfaces underfoot — you must be sure-footed and agile; possible route-finding problems in poor visibility

While there are more **waymarks** and signposts now than when the first edition of this book was published, Jersey still does not have an extensive system of public footpaths. Privacy is a cherished commodity on the island, and attempts to create long-distance routes have been thwarted due to landowners' reluctance to grant access.

The **1:25,000 maps** in this book are based on Openstreetmap mapping (see page 2), but have been very heavily annotated from our notes and GPS work in the field. We hope that these maps, which we have found to be *very* accurate on the ground, will be a boon to walkers.

Free **GPS track** downloads are available for all our walks: see the Jersey page on the Sunflower website. Please bear in mind, however, that GPS readings should *never* be relied upon as your sole reference point, as conditions can change overnight. *But even if you don't use GPS,* our maps are now so accurate that you can easily compare them with Google Maps on your smartphone and pinpoint your exact position. And it's great fun opening our GPX files in Google Earth to preview the walks in advance!

Below is a key to the symbols on our walking maps.

	main road		church.chapel	PH	pub, inn
	secondary road		cemetery.cross	WC	public toilets
	minor road/track		bus stop.parking	P	picnic (see page 9)
	rough track		water source, etc		best views
	footpath		ancient site.tower		castle.in ruins
2→	route of main walk and direction		windmill.aerial		page reference: map continuation
2→	alternative route		picnic tables	❶ ❷	waypoints
			watermill.tunnel		

Walk 1: ST HELIER HERITAGE

Distance: up to 3mi/5km; 1h30min-2h
Grade: 🟢 very easy
You will need: stout shoes, credit card (optional!)
How to get there: 🚌 or 🚗 to Pier Road (paycard required) [18].

The history of Jersey and its main town of St Helier is vivid and sometimes bloody. Jersey Tourism [1 on the plan; tel: 01534 859000] and the Jersey Museum are good places to start learning about the island.

Start out from **Liberation Square**: cross the open area to the **Jersey Museum** [3], with its distinctive clock face above the third storey arcades. Inside are paintings, furniture, maritime displays and Victoriana. Along with other relics, including her travelling case, there are two portraits of Jersey's famous actress daughter, Lillie Langtry, one of which is by Jerseyman Sir John Everett Millais. The Société Jersiaise (Jersey Society) next door has an excellent bookshop and

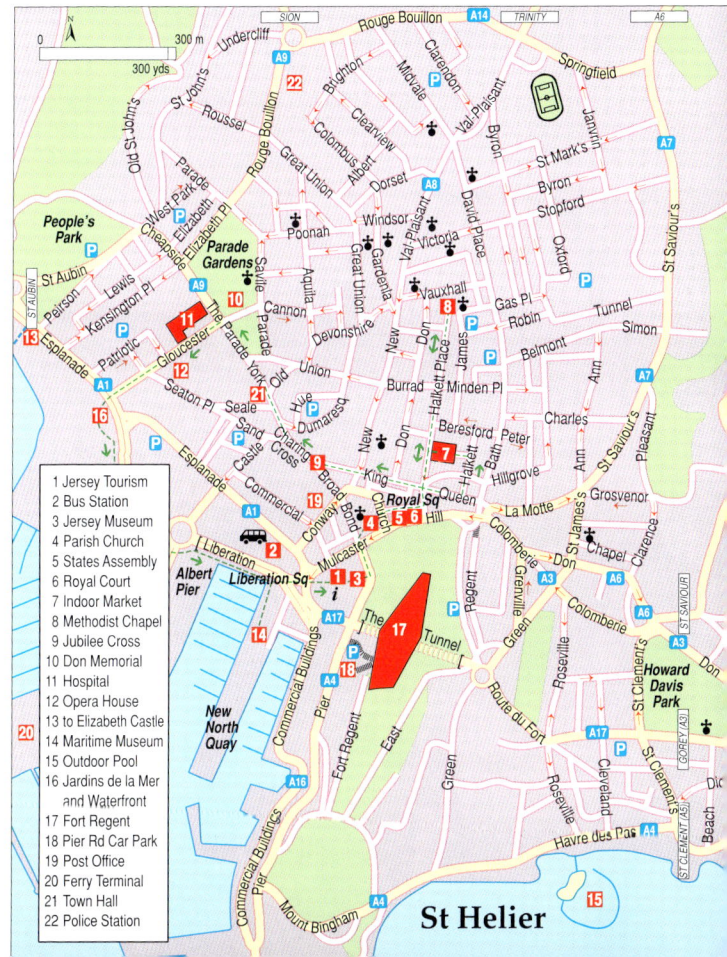

1 Jersey Tourism
2 Bus Station
3 Jersey Museum
4 Parish Church
5 States Assembly
6 Royal Court
7 Indoor Market
8 Methodist Chapel
9 Jubilee Cross
10 Don Memorial
11 Hospital
12 Opera House
13 to Elizabeth Castle
14 Maritime Museum
15 Outdoor Pool
16 Jardins de la Mer and Waterfront
17 Fort Regent
18 Pier Rd Car Park
19 Post Office
20 Ferry Terminal
21 Town Hall
22 Police Station

St Helier

library, and welcomes serious enquiries. Take steps from their office to Pier Road and walk down the hill to Mulcaster Street.

Then cross into Bond Street, to reach the west gate of **St Helier Parish Churchyard** [4]. According to legend, Helier was a 6th-century missionary who was murdered by pirates using axes, hence the symbolic crossed axes chosen as the emblem of the parish. The small chapel built on the rock where he lived near Elizabeth Castle became a place of pilgrimage known as the Hermitage. Walk through the churchyard (and indeed the church) and come to Church Street, once known as La Rue Trousse Cotillon or 'the street of raised petticoats' ... raised just enough for the ladies to cross what was once a filthy, muddy access to the Market Place, now known as **Royal Square**, which you are about to enter.

On the right are the **States' Assembly** [5; Jersey's parliament] and **Royal Court House** [6]. On the left there is an unusual wall-mounted sundial, and at the far end stands an imposing gilded statue of George II. In the far corner is the Peirson Inn (misspelled in the pub windows). It dates from 1749 but was named after Captain Peirson, who led a stirring victory over the marauding French on 6th January 1781, a day when Royal Square ran deep with blood. This

last serious attempt by the French to capture Jersey is recorded in a painting in the Tate Gallery, London, a copy of which hangs in the Royal Court. Just opposite the Peirson, note a fire insurance company mark on the wall of a jeweller's shop. In the early days of firefighting, your fire would only be put out if you had paid the premiums beforehand. No plaque? Well, then you had a conflagration, sir.

Leave the square near the pub, then turn right to reach the pedestrianised shopping zone of King Street/Queen Street. Turn right, then go left down Halkett Street, which brings you into Beresford Street where you should make a point of visiting the fish market — a feast for the eyes! Coming out, cross the street diagonally right to visit the main **Central Market** [7], which is a colourful melange of flowers, fruit, and vegetables surrounding a café and fountain.

There are many eateries around the market area: you can try a 'Jersey Wonder' from a bakery or sample Jersey ice cream or genuine Jersey products such as apple brandy or black butter (made from apples, not milk). And there are Italian, Portuguese, oriental, French and other restaurants to suit every taste. Leaving the market, come out into Halkett Place. Turn right and continue almost to the end of Halkett Place (crossing Burrard Street), to see the colourful façade of the **Methodist Chapel** [8] facing you at the end of the street. If you are a collector, you may like to know that you are now in a part of St Helier that is crammed with small shops and galleries, selling bric-a-brac, craft and off-beat items. From here walk back through Halkett Place to regain Queen Street.

Once back at Queen Street, turn right and walk along King Street shopping precinct to Charing Cross. Here you find a **granite cross** [9] commemorating the late Queen's Jubilee in 1977. Note its depiction of twelve aspects of Jersey life, from St Helier's Hermitage to a sailing ship, from a milk can to an ormer (the island's native shellfish delicacy). The surrounding flower bed is edged with granite blocks taken from

The indoor market in St Helier displays Jersey's produce at its finest. The central part, ranged round a lovely ornamental fountain, includes a café.

Elizabeth Castle and its causeway.

every quarry on the island and stone from the offshore reefs.

As you bear right along York Street to the **Town Hall** [21] — where there is a superb collection of paintings to be seen in the Assembly Room — you will see a pillar with a sculpted toad on top. The toad (*crapaud* in French) is the nickname — rudely given by Guernseymen — to island-born men. The road ahead passes the island's Cenotaph and widens into the Parade, with a fine **statue of General Sir George Don** [10] in the gardens near All Saints Church. He was a famous early 19th century Lieutenant-Governor known as 'the road-maker'.

Turn left into Gloucester Street, passing to the left of the **General Hospital** [11] and a nurses' home built on the site of the original Jersey prison (the present jail is on the coast east of La Corbière). On the left you'll see the **Opera House** [12], a fine Edwardian theatre restored in 2001 — definitely worth a visit.

Gloucester Street leads to the Esplanade, where you could turn right to get to the **causeway** [13] to Elizabeth Castle (Picnic 1), which starts almost opposite the Grand Hotel, but you might prefer to save this for a whole morning or afternoon. If you *do* walk over, be sure of the tides. (You can also make the trip in an amphibious 'ferry'. The Jersey Tourism office will tell you about the castle, which is well worth an excursion.)

Now cross the Esplanade safely at one of the pedestrian crossings with lights, to visit **Les Jardins de la Mer** [16] — beside La Frégate café, which is shaped like an upside-down boat. This seaside park has pebbled and paved walkways with a wonderful 'dolphin' fountain where children can play in a maze of water jets. Nearby is the **Waterfront** development, with garden areas, cafés and restaurants, a nightclub, gymnasium, apartments and a leisure pool with wave machine and beach area. The reclaimed land on which it is sited links the old harbours and modern ferry terminal via walkways through to **Albert Pier** and the lifeboat station. Walk on to the **Maritime Museum** [14] on New North Quay, from where you cross back to **Liberation Square** — ending the walk after **1h30min** to **2h**, depending on how long you've spent looking at the sights.

Walk 2: L'OUAISNÉ • ST BRELADE • BEAUPORT • LA LANDE DU OUEST • CORBIERE

See also photograph page 11
Distance: 8.4mi/13.5km; 3h40min
Grade: ● easy to moderate; there are some steep ascents/descents with steps on the paths near Beauport and around Corbière
You will need: comfortable shoes and long trousers (parts of the path may be overgrown with gorse). Binoculars could be useful.
Access: 🚌 12 or 12a to St Brelade's Bay and join the walk at St Brelade's Church, or 🚗 to L'Ouaisné (free) car park (49° 10.612'N, 2° 11.059'W).
Short walk: L'Ouaisné — Beauport — L'Ouaisné (4.5mi/7km; 1h40min; ● easy). Access as main walk. Follow the main walk as far as the headland overlooking Beauport and return the same way.
Alternative walk: ● link the walk with Walk 3 via the steeply stepped stony path that climbs up from L'Ouaisné beach to **Portelet Common**.

Strollers' corner (as I call it) is perfect for early morning or evening rambles, with some stunning scenery between Beauport and Corbière.

Starting at **L'Ouaisné** (pronounced 'Waynay'; ⭕) car park, head across the sands (tide permitting) or go along the edge of the common on the sea wall and up over **Le Grouin** point to **St Brelade's Church** (**25min**; ❶) at the far end of the bay, by the harbour. Parts of the church are Norman; the adjacent fishermen's chapel is thought to be of 12th-century origin. (In the southeast corner of the churchyard is the island's shortest sanctuary path *(perquage;* unfortunately gated and locked) — along which criminals could escape justice centuries ago, if they vowed never to return. Nearby is a viewpoint.)

Leave the churchyard by turning left out of the lych gate (opposite a sign on a wall, 'FOOTPATH TO BEAUPORT').

L'Ile au Guerdain in Portelet Bay once held the tomb of Philippe Janvrin, a sailor. He died from the plague in 1721, on a ship returning from France, and was initially buried here to minimise the risk of islanders contracting the disease.

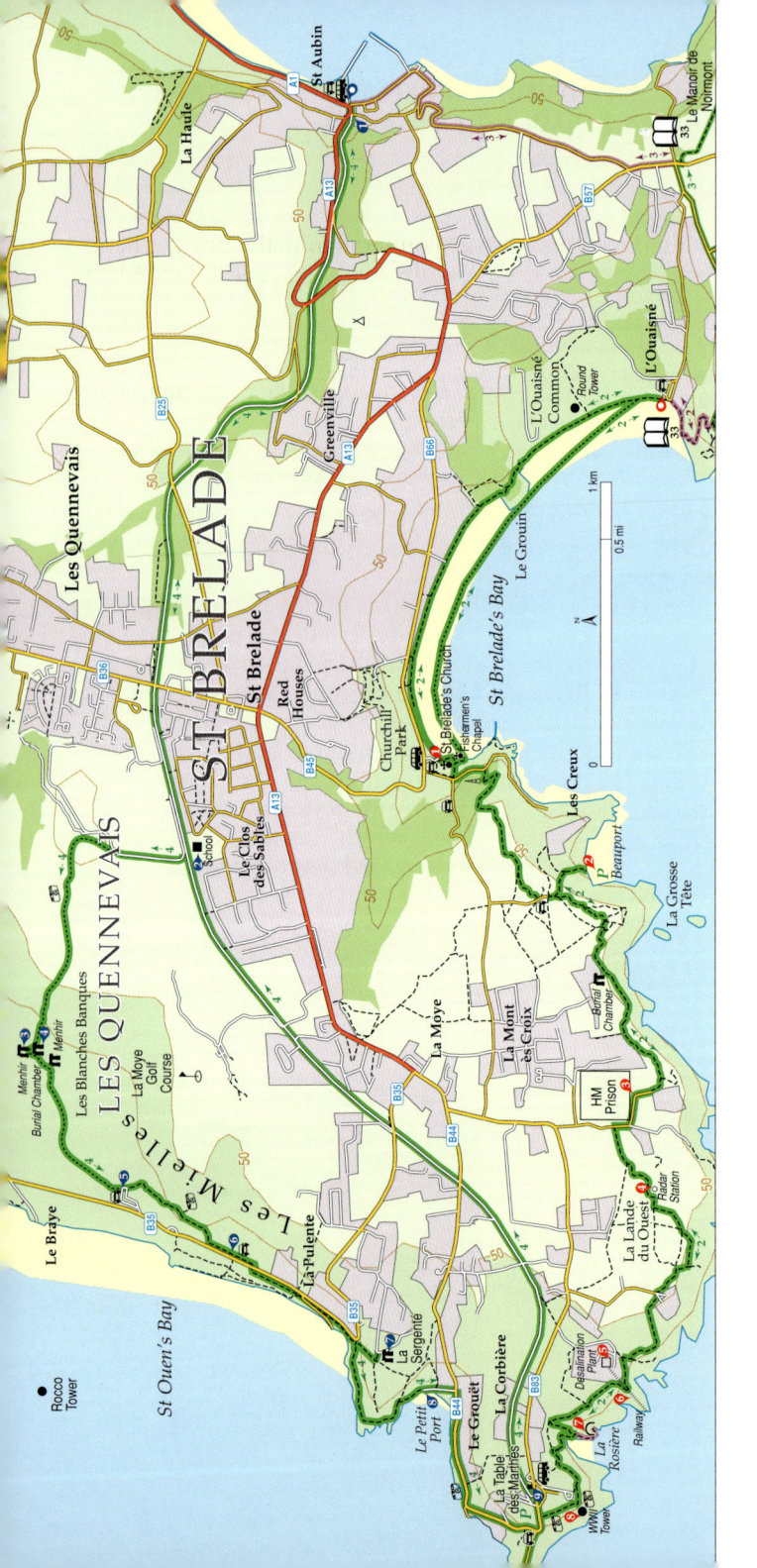

Walk 2: Circuit from L'Ouaisné to Corbière 31

Follow the road left uphill for 150 yards/metres, until a stone on the right indicates steps up the hillside and your ongoing path to **Beauport**. This is a quiet, unspoiled location with a very pretty beach (❷; **45min**; Picnic 2; photo on page 11).

Facing the sea, the path continues from the far right-hand corner of the car park. Take the right fork after just over 100 yards/metres. The path twists through patches of gorse, bracken and brambles and at times can be overgrown. At the stone marked 'LA GROSSE TÊTE' and 'LE CREUX', head right; after a few steps you will see another stone confirming you are on the coastal path. The next bit of the path is steep and with lots of steps.

When you reach the wall of a bungalow named 'Signal Point', turn right and walk a short distance to arrive at the perimeter fence of the island's **prison** (❸; **1h10min**). Here turn left on a road, then continue on the road as it turns right. Almost immediately you'll see the path (signposted) on your left — it passes a **meteorological radar station** (❹). Keep to the right of its tall tower, then turn left to follow a path back towards the cliffs, crossing the exposed, often breezy, common of **La Lande du Ouest**.

Eventually pass two houses on your left, then drop down below the **desalination works** built on the site of an old quarry (❺; **1h30min**). The path runs on the seaward side of the works, then upwards beside an inclined **narrow gauge railway track** (❻). Turn left as you reach the top and carry on along the cliff path. Soon you descend steep steps to a boulder-strewn beach, **La Rosière**. (A short detour on a path at the foot of the cliffs would take you to the mouth of a **cave**; ❼). Then more steps take you up to another headland with a **wartime tower** (❽). In a few minutes you will see **Corbière and its lighthouse** (❾), which you can visit at low tide.

When you reach the nearby bus stop (**1h50min**) you have the option of returning to St Brelade or back to St Helier by Bus 12, 12a or 22, shortening the walk by some 2mi/ 3km. (To extend the walk, perhaps link up with Walk 4.) Otherwise, retrace your steps to L'Ouaisné, using the sands or the promenade when you reach St Brelade, depending on the tide. At the end of the promenade, climb the steps to Le Grouin and ascend the hill either directly or via a gentler path to the right. Then follow a path down to the eastern half of the bay. It crosses private land, but walkers are welcome if they keep to the path. It passes an old tower and leads back to L'Ouaisné (❶; **3h40min**).

Walk 3: NOIRMONT AND PORTELET BAY

See also photo on page 15

Distance: 3mi/5km; 1h15min. (An optional extension to Portelet Beach adds at least 1mi/1.5km; 30-40min.)

Grade: ● easy, but the optional extension involves a fairly steep path and many steps to the beach at Portelet Bay, and a corresponding ascent — 200ft/60m.

You will need: comfortable shoes or trainers

Access: 🚐 12a to the Portelet terminus (Old Portelet Inn) or 🚗 to the (free) Portelet car park (49° 10.356'N, 2° 10.386'W). Return the same way.

Alternative walk: St Aubin — Noirmont — St Aubin (5mi/8km; 2h30min; ● grade as above). 🚐 12, 12a, 14 or 15 or 🚗 to St Aubin harbour (paycard required). Walk south along the harbour, then climb a narrow road, to join the walk described below at ❶, 25 yards/metres south of the crossroads by Le Manoir de Noir Mont. After visiting Noirmont, return the same way.

This is a fairly short circular walk, although if you take in the optional visit to Portelet Beach, you'll need stamina for the stiff climb back up the 'never-ending' steps. (You can, however, enjoy some fine views of St Aubin's Bay and Portelet Bay without descending to the beach.) After your walk — or before descending to the beach — the Old Portelet Inn is an ideal place to take on some sustaining refreshment.

With the **Old Portelet Inn** on your right, and the **car park/bus terminus** (❶) behind you, **start the walk** by taking the narrow road that runs along the front of the pub. It shortly passes a riding stable (also on your right), and just a couple of minutes from the pub you come to a junction with a block of apartments in view.

Turn right here, pass the apartments (now on your left), and continue to a T-junction. The large old Portelet Hotel used to stand just across the road, but was demolished in 2015. Turn left here and walk the short distance to **Portelet Common** (**15min**), for some stunning views over the bays of St Brelade and Ouaisné. This area, part of the National Trust for Jersey, is golden with gorse and purple with heather in the summer months. Take care — there are sheer drops around the old guard house and also over an old quarry face where a path comes up from Ouaisné. Make a circuit of the common (enjoying some excellent views of Portelet Bay) and, if you wish, walk through the gateway to enjoy the walk to **Le Fret Point**. Maybe you'll be spending about 20 minutes or so on the common, leaving it at about **35min**.

Return to the road, pass the site of the old Portelet Hotel on your left and continue until you reach another junction where a road climbs uphill from the left. Here you turn right. Be careful: the road is narrow, and there can be a fair amount of traffic (**45min**).

In under 100 yards/metres, you'll come to a crossroads. Turn right, and after 25 yards/metres take the signposted pathway on the left through a wooded area (❶). The path briefly passes through the woods, then you'll find yourself in semi-moorland, with huge clumps of gorse and broom, a glorious blaze of gold with a heady fragrance, especially in May and June. Avoid any bridleway here; the *main path has a netting fence on the left* which marks the boundary of the grounds of Le Manoir de Noirmont (private property, not open to the public). On your right you'll see many meandering side-paths along which you can wander if you are so inclined; they all eventually lead back to the main path, which you can recognise by the adjacent fencing.

A few minutes' walking will bring you to more open land, and you will see your destination in the distance. As you near **Noirmont car park** (❷), one of the preserved gun emplacements comes into view and, momentarily, you can visualise what the heavily-defended coast of the island looked like during the Second World War. Noirmont (the 'black hill'; Picnic 3) is a headland at the western end of St Aubin's Bay and is so named because it looms dark in certain conditions when viewed from St Helier.

You'll reach **two German guns** (**55min**), stark symbols of Jersey's dark days of Occupation. Even more stark is the **German bunker** built into the headland (shown overleaf), maintained as a museum by the Channel Islands Occupation Society. It is open occasionally during the summer and for group visits all year round, but if you want to visit it, do check opening times at ciosjersey.org because as each year passes, there seem to be a steadily decreasing number of enthusiasts needed to keep it open.

Spend a few more minutes in reflection while looking round the relics. From the main car park, walk back along

Some of the relics of the Occupation at Noirmont (see also photo on page 15).

the road which vehicles use to reach the headland. After some 250 yards/metres turn left on a footpath which will take you across to a **viewpoint** (**1h05min**) from which you can see Portelet Bay with L'Ile au Guerdain as its focal point.

Retrace your steps a short distance; then, instead of continuing on the path back to the car park, from the three-way fork take the path heading left (you approached from the right). This path will take you along the cliff-top to the Portelet car park and bus terminus and, of course, the **Old Portelet Inn** (**1h15min**).

If you want to extend the walk to **Portelet Beach**, look for a path on the seaward side, near the car park/bus terminus — it's signposted 'FOOTPATH TO THE BEACH' and you'll probably see a notice warning that there are no toilets on the beach. This diversion will take a minimum of half an hour. The path soon becomes steps. Once on the beach — depending on the state of the tide — you could also climb to the top of **L'Ile au Guerdain** (❸) and explore the tower marking the original site of Janvrin's tomb. (You'll see another path up from the beach a short distance to the right from the one by which you descended, but it's inadvisable to attempt returning by this path because although it would take you up to the top road, it passes through an area which is private property.)

By the time you've struggled back up the steps, you'll be more than ready to call in at the Old Portelet Inn (⊙) — for liquid or more sustaining refreshments!

Walk 4: THE CORBIÈRE WALK

See map on page 30; see also photos on pages 5 and 10
Distance: 8.7mi/14km; 3h30min **Grade:** 🟢 easy
You will need: stout shoes, sunhat, water in hot weather, binoculars
Access: 🚌 12, 12a, 14 or 15 or 🚗 to St Aubin harbour (49° 11.281'N, 2° 10.187'W; paycard required); return the same way.

It's a long time since a steam railway operated from St Helier via St Aubin, along the wide bay, to La Corbière lighthouse, one of Jersey's most visited landmarks. The old route makes an excellent, easy walk. I have varied the route from the signposted walk (extending the total distance slightly), to give you much finer views and a close look at a sand-dune environment, as well as some prehistoric standing stones. Birdwatchers could find this route a happy twitching-ground, for woodpecker and warbler, wader and finch.

Start out at **St Aubin harbour** (**O**): follow the road southwest as it turns inland, then take the first left then *immediately* right (**❶**; signposted for the **Corbière Walk**). Follow the walk for about 2mi/3km through pleasant woodland (crossing some roads), until **Les Quennevais School** (**❷**) is on your left (**50min**). On the right are its playing fields and beyond, the edge of **La Moye golf course**. Between them is a lane: follow it north a little way, under pine trees. You emerge with a skatepark on the right and sandy golf links on the left. Ahead is a good view of Jersey airport. Carry on for a few minutes, then turn left across the dunes (near a stile). There is no clear path: just choose the easiest way. This area is known as **Les Blanches Banques** and is of great interest to botanists who cherish its rare wild orchids and variety of grasses. It's part of the three-mile stretch of dunes known as **Les Mielles**. The dunes contain over 400 plant species including 15 rare species.

Ahead is the magnificent sweep of **St Ouen's Bay** (pronounced One's), and you will see Rocco Tower to the south of it. Look over the lower sandy plain towards the tower, and you should spot a **standing stone** (**❸**; menhir) — your next landfall. Head down from the upper dunes along the easiest route you can find and inspect the stone and a small nearby **burial chamber** (**❹**). Some of Jersey's many prehistoric sites are believed to have been associated with primitive forms of worship.

La Corbière lighthouse now lies south. Head towards it, across the lower dune area. You make easy progress now. Your first target is a **car park** (**❺**) with steps leading out of it past an old German bunker on the right. From here drop down to a **second car park** (**❻**) and, at the far end, cross the road.

Follow the roadside path to a sharp left bend. Here the main path curves right, round the base of a cliff, but you can first climb steps to the top of the cliff to see **La Sergenté** (3700 BC; ❼), the oldest tomb on Jersey. It's a private path with permitted access. The lower path (also private with permitted access) brings you round to **Le Petit Port** (❽; **1h40min**), a pretty bay offering shelter to a wide variety of birds, especially waders and warblers.

From here it's another 15-20 minutes along the road to **La Corbière** (Picnic 4) — spectacular in a winter south-westerly storm. If the tide is out, you can walk across the causeway to the lighthouse, but watch you don't get caught by the incoming tide (signalled by a siren)!

From the terminus near La Corbière you can catch bus 12, 12a or 22, timetable permitting. The main walk continues back to St Aubin: look out for a path on the left opposite the WC, as you walk up the road (signposted 'CORBIÈRE WALK'). It will bring you to the **old station** (❾). Facing the station (on the far side of the track), look out for the **Table des Marthes**. Popular myth has it that the great block of red granite is part of a prehistoric tomb and that, a hundred years ago, a contract signed on this stone was as binding as one made legally. To end the walk, now follow the track back to **St Aubin** (⓿; **3h30min**).

Sculpture near the Corbière lighthouse commemorating the rescue of passengers from the ferry St Malo in 1995

Walk 5: LE VAL DE LA MARE

Distance: 6.7mi/10.8km; 3h

Grade: 🔵 moderate, with a few steep (though short) sections

You will need: stout shoes, long trousers, sunhat, water in hot weather

Access: 🚌 9 (alight at New Road) or 🚗 to the (free) Val de la Mare car park on the A12 (49° 13.308'N, 2° 11.474'W); return the same way.

Short walk: Circuit of the Val de la Mare Reservoir (2.8mi/4.5km; 1h15min; 🟢 very easy). Access as above. Follow the main walk for 30min. Then climb up the other side of the valley and continue to skirt the reservoir. You will cross a causeway and enjoy fine views to St Ouen's Bay (Picnic 5b). On reaching your outgoing path, follow it back to the bus stop/car park.

This is the most varied of our walks, taking in a lovely reservoir circuit, a section of country park, and a Neolithic burial chamber. It will not seriously challenge experienced walkers, but has one or two steep sections.

Start the walk at the **bus stop/car park** on the A12 (⭕): take the waymarked path to the **Val de la Mare Reservoir** (built in the 1960s; **15min**). Bear left here (you will return from the right), and follow the waterside path round to the 100ft/30m-high **dam** (❶) and from there descend to the valley floor at the foot of the dam (**30min**). *(Those doing the Short walk continue up the other side of the valley, to circle the reservoir.)*

Follow the reservoir road seawards to reach Rue de Val de la Mare. Here turn right for about 1mi/1.3km, to the junction with Mont Matthieu (a road) on your right. (Those interested in wartime relics might wish to make a short

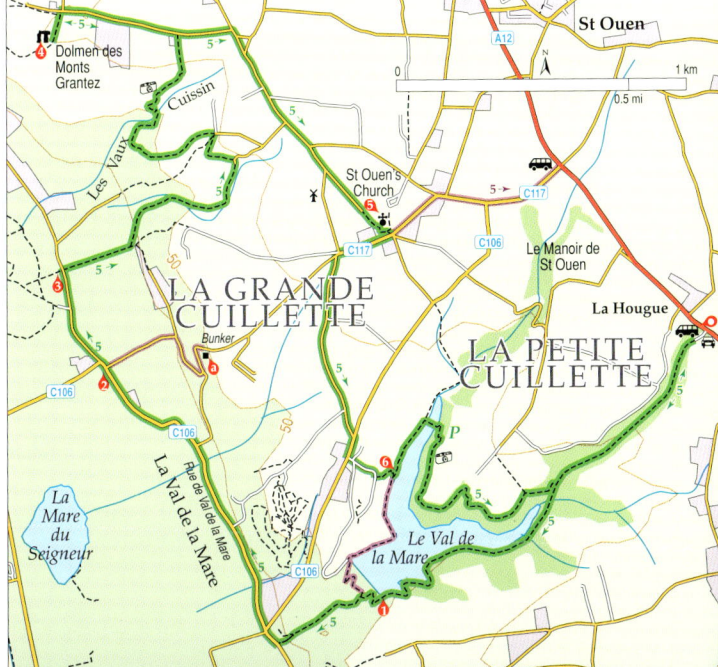

Picnic 5b: Le Val de La Mare Reservoir, with St Ouen's Bay in the distance

detour (❷) some 600 yards/metres up this road, to the neglected remains of one of a very few wartime bunkers bearing original German Bauhaus style lettering cast in concrete: GESTEINSBOHR KOMP 77. The **bunker** (❸) is on the right. Allow half an hour extra for this detour, marked in violet on the map.)

Under 400 yards/metres beyond the Mont Matthieu turning, go up a wide unsurfaced **sandy track** on the right (❸; **1h**) — *not* the surfaced track (Les Charrières à Sablon) shortly after, which leads to houses. After some 240 yards/metres come to a junction of paths with a waymark bearing the traditional acorn symbol. Here turn left — it was originally an old donkey trail dating from the time when *vraic* (seaweed) was used by farmers as a fertiliser. The path veers right and goes uphill. You'll pass by a pond on your right (it could be hidden behind bushes, depending on the time of year) and arrive at a house named La Ville au Bas (**1h20min**).

Turn left here and follow a wider, but still rough track for a short distance, until you arrive at a junction. Ignore a bridle path coming up from the left at 45° and make a 90° left turn to follow the waymarked route. It soon loops round and descends along the edge of a field into a valley, **Les Vaux Cuissin** (named on a small plaque on the left). Beyond a sometimes overgrown section you cross a little wooden bridge over a stream, then rise up to more fine views. Soon there are glasshouses over to your right and a high privet hedge alongside you, as you reach a metalled road, Le Chemin des Monts. Turn left for about 350 yards/metres, from where the **Dolmen des Monts Grantez** (❹) is

The path down to Les Vaux Cuissin. In the distance, fine views of St Ouen's Bay stretch from Corbière to Le Pulec.

accessible across a field on your left. It's one of the more substantial prehistoric graves on the island; uncovered in 1912, it yielded several 5000-year-old skeletons. The National Trust for Jersey owns this area, so you are free to wander down paths to **L'Etacq** and **St Ouen's Bay**.

Retrace your steps back to the road. Turn right and keep straight on past the house named Les Vaux Cuissin (where you came onto Le Chemin des Monts). When you come to a T-junction, turn right and Walk on for 600 yards/metres, to a Y-fork with an old **windmill** to the right of the right-hand fork. Take the left fork, a lane marked 'dead end', and follow it to **St Ouen's Church** (**5**; **2h10min**). (From here you could walk about half a mile east to St Ouen's Manor crossroads, to pick up Bus 8 or 9.)

The main walk continues by turning right from the main door of the church. Then take the first left into La Rue de la Campagne, walking past fields still strip-farmed as in medieval times. At a road junction, turn right, then very soon bear left on a track signposted to the Val de la Mare Reservoir. Take the left fork in the track and, at a small car park, go through a gate and descend a narrow path to the **edge of the reservoir** (**6**).

Turn left to follow the path round this arm of the reservoir, cross a **causeway** and climb up to enjoy splendid views towards St Ouen's Bay, with the airport over to your left. There are seats here, and grassy slopes which make an excellent picnic spot (Picnic 5b). Fifteen minutes later you reach your outward route; follow it back to the **Val de la Mare** bus stop/car park (**○**; **3h**).

Walk 6: THE PINNACLE

See also cover photo and see map of the north coast on the reverse of the touring map. You can easily link this walk with Walk 7 if you wish.

Distance: 3mi/5km; 1h30min

Grade: ● moderate; the ascent is steeper from L'Etacq

You will need: stout shoes, binoculars

Access: You can begin this walk at either Grosnez or L'Etacq. 🚌 8 to Grosnez or 🚗 to the free car park (49° 15.410'N, 2° 14.735'W); 🚌 12a, 22 or 🚗 to the free car park at L'Etacq (49° 14.433'N, 2° 14.952'W; also the L'Etacq bus terminus); return the same way.

Witchcraft and pagan rituals have made their mark on Jersey's history. While researching this book, I exercised my usual traveller's curiosity at most relevant sites, without being turned into a toad or even faintly discomfited. But there *is* something disturbing about this particular wind-swept cliff-top, with its Nazi detritus and the claustrophobic amphitheatre. See what you think. For good measure there's Grosnez 'Castle', the ruins of a 14th-century defence against the French who were demonstrably given to looting, pillaging, arson, rape, and murder on many a bloodthirsty 'away-day'.

So you tread on interesting soil. **Start out** at either Grosnez or L'Etacq. From **Grosnez** (**O**) just follow the cliff-top path south, towards a **German observation tower** (**❶**). From **L'Etacq** (**a**) climb the steep road behind the car park, passing the view shown on the cover, to pick up the sign-posted path to the top of the cliff; you pass some bunkers and many other wartime relics, some rusting away, others looking almost as when they were built.

The 200ft/60m-high Pinnacle rock, **Le Pinacle** (Picnic 6) looks benign enough on the approach (**❷**; **30min** from Grosnez; **20min** from L'Etacq). Neolithic man once used the local rock and flints to fashion tools, including ceremonial axes. Earlier generations worshipped here, drawn, one imagines, by the face of the rock. (Come here in the early morning and see the almost human 'face' thrown into shadowy features by the sun as it rises above the rim of the cliff!) The natural amphitheatre must have swarmed with superstitious islanders who created the shrine at the base some 2,000 years ago. Today, this important archaeological site is suffering from erosion, so please do not descend from the cliff-top, because the cliff is crumbling, continually eroded by the sea.

There are splendid views along the whole coastline. After you have walked from Grosnez to L'Etacq (or vice versa), you can vary your return route by taking paths slightly inland (see

Walk 6: The Pinnacle

suggested route on the walking map on the reverse of the touring map). You will skirt **Les Landes racecourse** (❸), where there are several meetings each summer, and pass a **rifle range** (❹) and an **airfield for model aircraft** (❺). Whichever route you choose, you should be back at your transport in **1h30min**.

Picnic 6: from the distance, the towering mass of the Pinnacle does not look too formidable. However, the mighty stack will one day stand in isolation — the sea has undermined the cliff, which is now rapidly eroding. So, for your own safety, content yourself with admiring it from the cliff top!

Walk 7: THE NORTH COAST

See map on the reverse of the touring map; see also photographs on pages 14 and 16. You can link this walk with Walk 6 if you wish.

Distance: up to 17mi/27.5km; 7h30min (beginning at Grosnez). The walk is best done in *at least* two days, breaking at Bonne Nuit Bay.

Grade: ● quite strenuous in places — *very strenuous* if done all in one go, with ups and downs of about 3300ft/1000m overall!

Equipment: stout shoes or light boots, tide table, binoculars, sun hat, picnic, water

Access: 🚌 bus links from and to St Helier at various points (see text for details of route numbers). At each point on the coast which you can reach by bus, the coastal path is very close to the bus stop. In many instances you will be able to see the path as you alight but, if you are in any doubt, ask at a kiosk or café and they will tell you where you can join the path. Or start by 🚗 and take a bus back to your parking place, but be aware that this will often involve taking a bus back to St Helier in order to get a bus or taxi from there back to where you left your car — on some routes this could take a couple of hours or more.

I have known masochistic walkers capable of devouring the whole of Jersey's coastline (about 40mi/65km) in a single trek. But they would have seen nothing, except the path ahead. You can 'do' the whole coast, seeing much more, but perhaps taking a week over it and gaining infinitely more pleasure from your exertions.

Some stretches of the coast have been introduced in earlier walks, and other admirable rambles can be made without guidance — for instance between St Helier and St Aubin, Green Island and Gouray on the east coast, or on the flat but atmospheric route skirting St Ouen's Bay on the west coast.

But in this 'chapter' we'll look at Jersey's north coast, with its towering cliffs, sea caves accessible at low tide, wooded valleys, and stunning views over perilous reefs towards Guernsey and the other Channel Islands — and, at the eastern end, to France on a clear day.

You don't need a mass of directions to follow a coastal path: broadly speaking, if you move too far to one side you'll lose sight of the sea; too far the other way and you'll fall into it. Where the way ahead needs a pointer, you have one, as there are wooden signs and stone waymarks all the way along the coast.

So I will offer a guide to key stages on the 15mi/24km (approximately) of beautiful coast that stretches between Grosnez in the west (Walk 6) and Rozel in the east (Walk 9). It makes sense to me to divide this stretch into at least two days. Nowhere is it really difficult, and at several points you can escape by bus, take refreshment, or divert temporarily to other attractions.

Begin the walk at **Grosnez** (**○**; 🚌 8, 9 or 🚗). (If you

The waterfall cave at Plémont

use the bus, you'll have about a third of a mile to walk from the B55 before reaching Grosnez.) Heading east, the first port of call is **Plémont** (**1**; 1.5mi/2.5km; **45min**; 🚌 8), with lovely views over La Grève au Lançon beach. There's a waterfall cave *(no access)* running under the beach café, and you'll also see Needle Rock.

Next is **La Grève de Lecq** (**2**; 4mi/6.5km; **2h**; 🚌 9), where the Moulin de Lecq pub has a waterwheel in the bar and you can visit the 19th-century barracks described on page 16. There's also another excellent beach to explore and a choice of refreshment options. Climb the path indicated near the **old barracks** for about 0.6mi/1km, then detour round a **shooting range** (the route varies depending on whether firing — indicated by red flags — is in progress). Come to **Le Col de la Rocque** (**a**), a splendid headland viewpoint.

Shortly reach **Devil's Hole** (**3**; 6mi/10km; **3h**; 🚌 7) and a decent pub — the Priory. You pass a huge statue of the Devil rising out of a pool as you take the path down to the **cave** (**b**), shown on page 14. There's a steepish flight of steps at the end of the path, a peculiar cave with a blow-hole through which the sea crashes and the views reward your exertions. In 2006 this area was given to the National Trust for Jersey.

Retrace your steps to the main path and continue along another headland, then descend into **La Vallée des Mouriers** (**c**) and climb out again for more excellent views. To the north, a mile or two offshore, lie the perilous rocks of Paternoster Reef. Walk 8 also follows this stretch of path, which leads to a superb viewpoint at **Sorel** (**d**) but then has to leave the coast to avoid **Ronez Quarry** (**e**). This diversion is well enough signposted. The path continues along the heights, following a road built by islanders during the occupation (a stone tablet opposite Les Fontaines pub records their efforts). Ahead you'll see the island's **television transmitter** (**f**), a slender 'Eiffel Tower'! When you reach the junction of the C101 with its **Millennium Cross**, walk a short way inland to the fascinating 'Farmhouse' bar and restaurant, where there's a pub located in an interesting old building.

Back on the path, you pass a **smaller quarry** (**3h50min**). From here you should be able to see kestrels, gulls, fulmar and the common shag perched on the offshore Cormorant Rock. Pass a one-time pub, now a private house (near Picnic 7a), and in ten minutes or so, come to **Frémont Point** (❾), from where you overlook the beautiful double sweep of Bonne Nuit and Giffard bays with Belle Hougue Point in the distance. Descend to **Bonne Nuit** (❹; 9km/14.5km; **4h30min**; 🚌 4), an ideal place to break, with a café by the pier and a bus stop ahead.

Opposite the bus stop is a steep hillside once grazed by sheep, now owned by the National Trust for Jersey; here you can enjoy spectacular views from a **circular path** (ⓑ; see map). The coast path resumes its way east now, passing between buildings — and above a massive landslip (2016), where the Cheval Roc Care Home almost disappeared over the cliff — before dividing into a lower and upper path. Either way will suit you; the best views are from the higher path. Beyond the headland of **La Belle Hougue** the paths combine again, leading past **Le Petit Port** (ⓘ; don't blink or you'll miss it) and through a lovely and equally *petit* bit of woodland, to come to **Bouley Bay** (❺; 12mi/19km; **6h**; 🚌 4 from Trinity Church; Picnic 7b).

Once a smugglers' haunt, and known to motor sport enthusiasts for its hill climb, Bouley is a picturesque bay framed by volcanic cliffs. Its steeply-shelving beach has been judged the cleanest in the UK, and there are superb underwater diving facilities. You can also take a side-stroll here if you wish, up to **Le Jardin d'Olivet**, scene of a battle with the French in the 16th century.

Continue from the Water's Edge Hotel to arrive at delightful **Rozel** (❻; 15mi/24km; **7h30min**; 🚌 3; Walk 9). Before boarding your bus enjoy some refreshments here; the 'Hungry Man' kiosk on the pier is justly famous for its home-made food.

Walk 8: SOREL AND LA VALLEE DES MOURIERS

See map on the reverse of the touring map; see photograph opposite
Distance: 2mi/3km; 1h
Grade: ● moderate; the cliff path is occasionally rough, with some short steep sections and lengthy stretches of steps
You will need: stout shoes
Access: 🚌 to Sorel (49° 15.443'N, 2° 9.482'W); two free car parks
Alternative walk: Circuit from St John's Church (5mi/8km; 2h30min; grade as above). 🚌 5 or 7 to St John's Church. Follow the C101 and C100 to the viewpoint at Sorel, then continue the main walk, before returning to St John's.

This short circular walk takes in farm land, a peaceful wooded valley, and a stretch of cliff path with fine views and good picnic spots overlooking the sea.

Start out at **Sorel** (**O**), a breezy headland adjacent to the busy **Ronez granite quarry**. Walk a few hundred yards/metres back along the road you followed to reach the viewpoint. When you reach the T-junction (with Sorel farm facing you), turn right. Follow the road round the farm buildings (they will be on your left) and keep with it as it takes a right-hand turn. Now, stay on this road, passing one or two houses and occasional roads and paths joining from the left. Still on the same road, at **15min** pass a junction on your left with a 'Give way' sign and soon start going downhill.

Come to a junction where there is a turning off to the right, and soon after, another to the left; ignore them both. When you reach the bottom of the hill, you will find yourself at a small crossroads (**25min**). Here, turn right, taking the road that runs along the left-hand side of a stream, the start of which may be hidden by weeds and foliage.

Now you come to the best part of the walk. Your route descends through the **Vallée des Mouriers** towards the sea. When the road you are on bends left and sweeps uphill past a cottage on your left, take a track that forks away to the right directly opposite the cottage. Pass a small **reservoir** on your right (**35min**). Shortly before you reach the sea (there's no beach, just a rocky shelf), look to the right for the coastal path and join it (Walk 7 also follows this section — this is waypoint (**O**) in Walk 7 on the map).

From here on, it's just a matter of following the cliff path which, though narrow in parts, is not hazardous, provided that the ground is dry underfoot. Look out for the grazing herd of Manx Loaghtan sheep which assist with conservation management; fencing and stiles have been introduced to contain them. In **1h** the path brings you back to **Sorel** (**O**).

Left: the coastal path near Sorel (Walks 7 and 8)

Walk 9: AROUND ST MARTIN AND ROZEL

See also photographs pages 2 and 20
Distance: 6.3mi/10.2km; 3h
Grade: ● moderate; after a rainy spell, the woodland paths can be muddy. The path between Rozel and Le Havre de Scez (via the Dolmen du Couperon) is also both stony and rather steep in short stretches.
You will need: stout shoes or walking boots
Access: 🚌 2 or 🚗 to the car park at St Catherine's Tower, south of the La Maison slipway (49° 13.112'N, 2° 1.784'W; free but limited space)

This delightful inland walk takes you through woodland and along quiet country roads and paths flanked by carpets of wild flowers. It also visits the seaside village of Rozel and the Dolmen du Couperon.

From **St Catherine's Tower** (**○**), **start out** by turning left and walking up the road, away from the sea. When you reach the crossroads, turn right along the one-way road marked with a 'no entry' sign (for vehicles). Almost immediately, fork left on a track that leads to Rozel woods. This stony track first takes you past a small private fishing **pond** (**❶**) which began life as a German-built reservoir during the Occupation. It then leads into **Rozel Woods** (Picnic 9), across two lots of stepping stones and alongside a pretty stream. This is the habitat of birds like the great spotted woodpecker, also the red squirrel, the latter a rare creature now on the British mainland.

Follow the path for about **20min**, ignoring another path which joins it from the left (**❷**; the old *perquage* or 'sanctuary path' from St Martin, down which in days gone by villains could legitimately flee the island if they promised never to come back!).

In just over 100 yards/metres, come to a T-junction of paths and go left. The path now climbs fairly steeply out of the woods. After another 250 yards/metres it becomes surfaced with tarmac and bends left, to take you past a property on your left. As the buildings end, turn right. Walk along a lane which passes through farming land. You'll see on your left a huge **multi-sided construction** (**❸**) surmounted by a lot of mushroom-shaped domes. It looks like some enormous spacecraft that has just landed, but is part of the airport's navigational aids. You are now nearly at St Martin. A few minutes later, come out into Rue de Belin, where the **Methodist Chapel** (**❹**) is on your right. Pass the chapel and, within a few yards/metres emerge on the **main B38 road** (**40min**), where you turn right. (If you want to make a detour to the centre of the village of St Martin and the church, turn left instead, but make sure you return to take up the route from this spot.)

After ten minutes you cross a stream (though you may not be able to see any water for all the trees). Five minutes later turn left at a T-junction. Soon you will have a good view of St Martin over to the left. Ignore a turning to the left. Then, some 200 yards/metres further on (near a postbox set in a wall), turn right into Rue du Moulin. You may be able to glimpse the **tower** (**5**) shown at the left, the remains of one of Jersey's oldest windmills. Set in private grounds, it is a fine sight. Follow the road down through a narrow one-way system, dropping into **Rozel Valley** and turning right at a T-junction to reach **Rozel Bay** (**6**; **1h15min**).

Rozel is a lovely place to linger (the Hungry Man kiosk on Rozel pier is highly recommended for a snack) but, to continue the walk, climb the road, with superb

Left: Le Moulin de Rozel; below: the Dolmen du Couperon. In the background, beyond Le Havre de Scez beach, is La Coupe, a small headland topped by a little tower.

views to your left over the harbour. At the top of the hill, look out back to your left for a sign reading 'Public footpath to Le Scez' and take this path, which drops steeply with fine views over Rozel and the inlet of Le Douët de la Mer. The path twists and turns, drops and climbs, reaching **Le Couperon**, the prehistoric burial site shown opposite — just a few yards/metres to your left (**7**; **1h40min**). It is one of only two gallery graves in Jersey.

Continue downhill for a few yards/metres, to the end of Rue des Fontenelles. ('Rue' is rather an overstatement here and elsewhere in Jersey, where it describes even the most humble of paths.) At this point you will see a small car park and a path running off to the left of the main car park. This leads down to **Le Havre de Scez** (a sheltered anchorage rather than a harbour), where seaweed for fertilising the land was once collected. It's a pleasant and sometimes-deserted beach.

From here, you can see the sentry tower at the top of La Coupe, which you will visit a little later in the walk. Go up the narrow road which twists and turns steeply uphill (it won a competition for the 'most scenic lane' in Jersey). Further up, a sign proclaims that the lovely area on your left is owned by the National Trust for Jersey. Unfortunately no paths run through it, and you must keep to the road.

The road soon veers quite sharply to the left and then levels out; take the first turning to the left. Follow this road down an increasing gradient until you reach **La Coupe** (**8**; **2h05min**), the promontory shown in the lower photo on page 48. There is access to a small beach down a path on the right.

Then climb back up the same road until you reach the T-junction. Turn left, following the road as it twists right, then left, as far as a crossroads *(where Walk 10 comes in from the left)*. Go straight across and, not far beyond a riding centre on your right, turn into a road that forks back to the right (signposted 'LES MARES'). This passes between a few buildings and rapidly becomes a narrow farm track leading down to **Rozel Woods**. At the point where it changes to a hard surface and becomes walled on both sides, look across to the right for a fine view of Rozel Manor (**9**).

Continue down the track and come back to the junction where, earlier in the walk, you turned left to climb out of the woods and up to St Martin's. From here, turn left to retrace your steps past the stretch of water on your left, back to the car park at **St Catherine's Tower** (**O**; **3h**).

Walk 10: A SHORT STROLL AROUND FLICQUET

See map on page 47
Distance: 2mi/3km; 1h
Grade: ● very easy, with just a couple of ascents (one steep and stony)
You will need: comfortable shoes or trainers
Access: 🚌 2 or 2a or 🚗 to St Catherine's Bay (49° 13.476'N, 2° 1.184'W; ample free parking); return the same way.

Motorists often like to break their driving with a circular walk of a couple of miles. This one is ideal: it's often overlooked by those who park at St Catherine's Bay and, wanting a breather, simply walk to the end of the breakwater and back. The breakwater, a 850yd/800m-long granite structure, was built in the mid-1800s as the start of what was to have been a major harbour. However, before completion it was realised that it would be hopelessly silted up most of the time, so the Admiralty just finished its construction to save face.

Start out at **St Catherine's Bay** (◉) by walking back, along the loop road you've just used, but against the traffic. In less than 100 yards/metres past the café and toilets, look out for a level path on the right-hand side of the road, signposted 'FOOTPATH TO FLIQUET'. This starts out as a steep and stony climb, but almost immediately you have to bear right to avoid a landslip in 2014 (❶), when the path was closed for a time.

Around here you may still see the bits of war-time history shown opposite: two sets of anti-tank barriers which were erected by the German Occupation forces. They consist of lengths of railway track — a relic of Jersey's long defunct railways — embedded vertically in the pathway. As you near the top of the hill, look out for a waymarked post on your right and turn right into a field

Walk 10: A short stroll around Flicquet 51

with many trees. (There is a seat from which you can enjoy the view; it also makes a pleasant picnic spot.) The grassy path through the field soon brings you out on a secluded road. Here turn right and walk down the hill to the quiet little cove at **Flicquet**, with its ancient defence tower (❷).

Pass the tower and continue along the road, which starts to climb gently. Soon you'll come to a pseudo-Spanish style house, a 20th-century folly built beside the road, on your left. The road takes a sharp hairpin bend to pass three sides of this unusual residence, then curves upwards past an attractive row of cottages set back on the right. The flowers surrounding these cottages can be spectacular if you pass by at the right time of the year.

Continue along the road, which is quiet and unlikely to have any traffic, apart from an occasional car seeking one of the very few parking spaces at tiny Flicquet. Pass a bungalow on your left; it appears to be built entirely from wooden tiles. At **25min** you reach a junction where Walk 9 comes in from the right: turn left. (Or, if you would like to extend your walk by half an hour, instead turn right, follow the road as it makes a sharp turn to the right and then to the left. Then, within a few yards/metres, take a road to the right and follow it for about a third of a mile (500m), to the little headland of La Coupe shown on page 48. Retrace your steps to pick up the main walk again.)

In company with Walk 9, head south along this road, where the hedgerow is sometimes a mass of colourful flowers. Soon pass riding stables on the right and then a road off to Les Mares (where Walk 9 turns off to the right). In another 150 yards/metres, take the road on the left signposted to Flicquet. Pass minor turnings on both sides of the road until, after half a mile (800m) of gentle descent, the road takes a sharp turn to the left. Just at the point where it bends, take the track leading downhill to the right.

Start down the Flicquet footpath, then descend steps on the left to avoid the landslip. Rejoin your outward route and turn right. At the bottom of the hill, follow the road back to **St Catherine's Bay** (०) and breakwater — ready, no doubt, for lunch or a cream tea (**1h**).

Wartime relics on the Flicquet pathway

Walk 11: ST CATHERINE'S TO GOREY

See map page 47 and photograph pages 12-13
Distance: 3mi/5km; 1h15min
Grade: ● easy
You will need: stout shoes
Access: 🚌 2 or 2a to St Catherine's Bay. Return on 🚌 1, 1a, 2 or 13 from Gorey to St Helier. Alternatively, 🚗 park at St Catherine's Bay (49° 13.476'N, 2° 1.184'W; ample free parking) and after the walk retrace your steps to St Catherine's Bay (2h30min-3h30min).

Alternative walk: Flicquet — St Catherine's Bay — Gorey (5mi/8km; about 2h15min). Do Walk 10, then follow up with this walk.

Short though it is, this linear walk packs a variety of scenery into a few leisurely miles along the east coast. It starts at St Catherine's breakwater — a major harbour that never was; see page 50. It's about a mile out and back, if you wish to walk it first.

Start out by walking back along the main road you took to reach **St Catherine's Bay** (**O**), using the path along the seaward side of the road. Pass **La Maison slipway** and **St Catherine's Tower** (also **O** — starting point for Walk 9) and two picnic areas with barbecues (Picnic 11a). Then come to the 18th-century **Archirondel Tower** (**❶**; **35min**) on a short breakwater. Just beyond it is Archirondel Beach: not too crowded, it makes a fine picnic spot.

Leave the path here: go down to the beach and for a short distance walk on the pebbles. Then climb the third flight of steps you come to and follow a short path through a small field to the coast road (**50min**).

Turn right on the road (or go left for Picnic 11b). Almost immediately, go left on Rue des Puchots, climbing quickly to a T-junction, where you turn left (but *not* into Mont de la Crete, which is also on the left within a few paces). Keep walking, ignoring side turnings, until you come to a T-junction with a signpost pointing right to the '**Dolmen de Faldouët**, 15yds'. This 50ft/15m-long prehistoric passage grave (**❷**; **1h**) has a capstone reckoned to weigh over 20 tonnes.

Return to the road and bear right for some 200 yards/metres, to a distinct U-bend. The first opening on the bend leads to an aerial. Walk along it briefly, to get some marvellous views over Gorey Bay towards Gorey's Castle, before returning to take the next road on your left: this takes you down to the coast road, almost opposite **Mont Orgueil Castle** (**❸**; **1h15min**). Visit the castle if you've time, or turn right and walk down to the shops and cafés of **Gorey** before catching your bus back to St Helier. Or retrace your steps to **St Catherine's Bay** (**O**; **2h30min**).

Walk 12: ST LAWRENCE: THE HEART OF JERSEY

Distance: 4.8mi/7.5km; 2h40min
Grade: ● moderate, but with a few short steep sections
You will need: sensible shoes, long trousers
Access: 🚌 7 or 7a to St Lawrence's Church or 🚗 (49° 12.906'N, 2° 8.476'W; ample roadside parking near the church parish hall)

Alternative, longer walk: St Lawrence circuit and the Jersey War Tunnels (9.6mi; 15.5km; *allow 5h-6h30min*; moderate; access as above). This walk is easily linked with Walk 13. Follow this walk to the crossroads at the 2h15min-point (just before ❸). Instead of turning left, go straight on here, then turn right after a couple of minutes where the road divides. Now keep straight on to join the start of Walk 13 at the Jersey War Tunnels, which are shown in the bottom left-hand corner of the map. After Walk 13, retrace your steps to the crossroads and turn *right*, past ❸, to complete this walk.

This walk is a circular route winding along sheltered country roads, 'green lanes' and footpaths in the heart of Jersey. Before setting off, the parish church of St Lawrence is worth a visit; it stands on high ground and has a distinctive outline with a saddle-back roof to its tower. Just to the north of the church is the parish hall.

Start out at **St Lawrence**: take the lane with the 'no through road' sign, opposite the **parish hall** (**○**) and war memorial. This descends very steeply down **Mont Misère** (Misery Hill), into the picturesquely-wooded St Lawrence Valley — known locally as '**Waterworks Valley**' on account of the reservoirs running the length of its stream (**15min**).

Reaching the bottom of Mont Misère, you will see your route on your left, just below road level — the wooden zigzag boardwalk shown overleaf. But before setting off along this path, cross the road and follow a signposted footpath to the right for some 100 yards/metres. Beyond a pump house, in a clearing among splendid horse chestnut trees, is the **St Lawrence Millennium Standing Stone** (❶; one of twelve — there is one in each parish) and an information board which explains the natural history of the area and how a team of volunteers created a new '**Millennium Path**' to celebrate the year 2000. (The path continues down the valley, to Millbrook Reservoir further downstream, and also links up with 'green lanes' leading to St Helier — an option you might like to explore another day.)

Now retrace your steps to the zigzag boardwalk (also part of the Millennium Path) and follow it over the water meadow. Soon you cross a bridge and then climb 70 steps to a **viewpoint** among the tree-tops, high above **Dannemarche Reservoir**, from where you can look out across the narrow valley. This sheltered little eyrie is filled with wild flowers and bird-song in spring, full of butterflies in summer, and carpeted with fallen leaves and chestnuts in autumn.

54 Landscapes of Jersey

Depending on the season and time of day, you may get a glimpse of a red squirrel.

The path descends and returns to the road (**50min**). Turn left and continue along the valley for less than 100 yards/metres — until you see a narrow passageway cut through bedrock on the left. This is the path, and you will cross more bridges as it twists among trees and lush vegetation — ferns, honeysuckle and prickly butchers' broom and gorse. Beyond a grassy roadside picnic area with parking (**1h05min**), the route continues by crossing the road and running along the edge of a meadow.

Walk up to see the buildings of the **Hamptonne Country Life Museum** (❷; open year round, check opening times and prices by calling 01534 863955). To get there, leave the path and follow the road to the left, straight up the hill for under 300 yards/metres, then turn right; you'll see them on your right. And be sure to take a look at the lovely *colombier* (dovecot) on the left at the top of the hill.

After your visit, retrace your steps to the path you were on and continue north. Cross a footbridge and go through

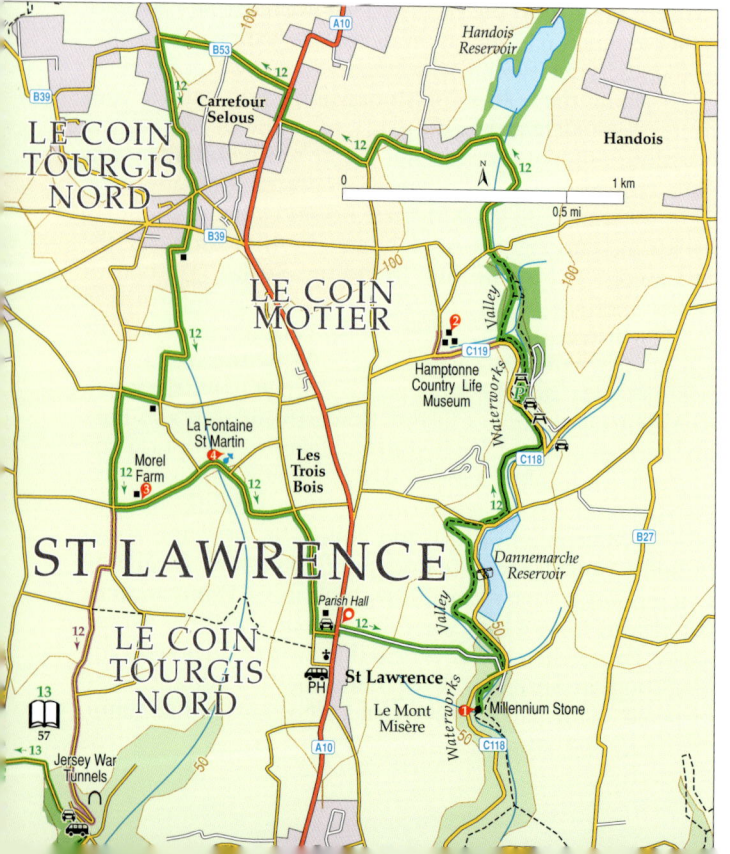

The zigzag boardwalk over the often marshy water meadow

a gate, once again crossing a road. With the stream beside you, the lane soon passes by an old **watermill** now converted into a house (**1h15min**).

From here the walk follows lanes, with a final stretch of pathway ending opposite another water-pumping station below yet another reservoir (the **Handois Reservoir**; **1h25min**). Follow the road as it winds to the left and ascends; at the top, take the turning on your right. On reaching the main road (A10) again, turn right and after about 100 yards/metres turn left, down Rue de la Golarde (**1h40min**). Turn left at the T-junction and enjoy the trees arching overhead (the 'tunnel' effect is dictated by ancient laws governing annual hedge-cutting). Go straight on for about 600 yards/metres — to a small crossroads, turn right for 20 yards/metres, then turn left into a tiny lane. Then cross almost straight over another road, the **B39** (**1h55min**).

Beyond the entrance to a manor house on the left, the lane twists and turns, passing an old water pump. Go straight on where the lane narrows, then turn right opposite a large farmhouse with a thatched and tiled roof. After 150 yards/metres, at a small crossroads among fields, turn left; then turn left again at the next crossroads (opposite Leda House; **2h15min**). On your left is **Morel Farm** (❸; National Trust for Jersey), with a rare cobbled yard — a timeless scene viewed through the arched gateway. Go on down the hill to Le Rat, a tiny cottage beside another stream which runs through a quiet valley. Look out for **La Fontaine St Martin** — a stone well beside the road (❹; **2h25min**).

Keep the meadow stream on your right as you go up a short steep hill and, at the next crossroads, turn right along another shady lane which will return you to the church at **St Lawrence** and the bus stop or your car (○; **2h40min**).

Walk 13: JERSEY WAR TUNNELS

Distance: 4mi/6.5km; 2h10min
Grade: ● easy
You will need: stout shoes
Access: 🚌 8 or 28 or 🚕 to Jersey War Tunnels (49° 12.599'N, 2° 9.264'W; ample free parking). (Bus users also have the option of returning by bus from the Victoria pub.)
Short walk: since this walk makes a figure of eight, a pleasant stroll of about half the length, mostly on footpaths, can be achieved by cutting out the loop north of the Victoria pub (❶), where you should turn *left* on the valley road.

First-time visitors to Jersey are often surprised to discover the extent and legacy of the five-year Occupation (1940-45). The story is no more vividly told than at the Jersey War Tunnels, a massive complex built when the Germans entrenched themselves in the Channel Islands, believing them to be stepping stones to a full invasion of the UK. A visit to the tunnels will amaze you. Hitler never felt the island sunshine himself, but his command HQ was not far away: we pass it on this walk. Everything remains as it was when the occupying forces left. This major tourist attraction vividly brings to life the incredible achievement of the architect and slaves who worked in appalling conditions to complete the project. The entry fee includes various multi-media exhibitions. The walk passes the entrance; allow extra time for this highly recommended visit.

Begin at the **Jersey War Tunnels** bus stop (⬤). Walk up Mont du Rocher, with a view to the museum entrance on your right. A minute or two later, follow the road as it makes a near-90° turn left, and come to a T-junction with Rue de la Ville au Bas. Turn left again, and after 150 yards/metres, go right, gently descending. Just after a sharp bend to the left, follow the footpath signs on the right to avoid the narrow (but busy) main road near the **Victoria pub** (❶; **25min**).

Go up the hill to the right *(the Short walk goes left on the valley road here)*. Continue on La Route de L'Aleval, passing (on your left) the entrance to a war-time tunnel. This was once Jersey's **main mushroom farm** (❷), but is now defunct (mushrooms are imported from Guernsey). Walk on the grassy verge at the edge of the road for about 0.6mi/1km; there are more tunnel entrances on both sides of the road, now blocked. You are on a road that was created by the German forces for access to their military headquarters.

Opposite: the corridors of Jersey War Tunnels extend for more than a kilometre and were constructed by forced labour between 1941 and 1943, initially as a bomb-proof munitions store and repair facility. Between late 1943 and 1945 the complex was converted into a clearing station for military casualties, which in the end was never used.

Walk 13: Jersey War Tunnels   57

Turn left at the top of the hill at Le Pissot (**50min**) and in 10 minutes reach the grounds of a now-defunct theme park called 'The Living Legend': the **nerve centre for the Occupation** (❸) was underground here. During the war the command bunker was disguised as a cottage; later it was incorporated into the theme park buildings as a storage area. Today this area is a housing estate. The walk continues by turning left just beyond the estate, on a fairly quiet road. Keep ahead until the road makes a sharp left turn and zigzags downhill, back to the **Victoria pub** (❶; **1h35min**).

Turn right and go along the valley road about 250 yards/metres, to the millpond (on your left). From here the walk continues on footpaths. First there is a path through National Trust for Jersey woodland to **Quetivel** (❹; **1h35min**), a restored water mill (open to visitors on Saturdays in summer). Across from the mill, the path goes through gateposts and continues downstream along the valley. Soon turn left to cross the stream, then go right along the roadside path as far as a **pumping station** (❺). Cross the road carefully here, then take the steep path on the other side. This winds its way through the trees, over the hill and down to your car or the bus stop at the **Jersey War Tunnels** (❶; **2h10min**).

Walk 14: GOREY VILLAGE AND QUEEN'S VALLEY

See map page 47
Distance: 4mi/7km; 1h55min
Grade: ● quite easy, with an initial climb of 200ft/60m
You will need: stout shoes (the reservoir paths are loose grit)
Access: 🚌 1, 1a, 1g or 2 to/from the terminus at Gorey (Gouray), or 🚗 to/from Gorey harbour (49° 11.984'N, 2° 1.297'W; paycard required)
Short walk: Queen's Valley Reservoir circuit (2mi/3km; 45min; ● easy). Walk around the lake; perhaps use the causeway to cross from one side to the other for a figure-of-eight. 🚌 13 to Queen's Valley (St Saviour's Hospital) or by 🚗 (49° 12.117'N, 2° 2.471'W; free parking at the St Saviour's Hospital end of the reservoir, or at the southern end).

Jersey's newest reservoir, resulting from the flooding of Queen's Valley, makes an enjoyable walk, because you can get around the entire lake on wide, mainly-level paths, encountering no traffic whatever. You'll also enjoy walking along quiet roads around Gorey.

Start out from the bus stop/car park in **Gorey** (**O**): walk up the B30 (St Martin's) road for under 200 yards/metres, but then take the U-turn to the right onto the coast road (B29). When you are just about level with Mont Orgueil Castle, turn left. (Immediately left at this junction is a granite stone inscribed 'T.R. DE GRUCHY, CONNETABLE 1931'.) Almost as soon as you've turned off the main road, ignore a cul-de-sac on the left; bear right, and stay on this road as it climbs quite steeply. You'll have magnificent views of the bay, the castle and also — on a clear day — the coast of Normandy. Ignore a left turn 'Public footpath and steps to Gorey village ½'.

A few minutes later arrive at a **junction** (**❶**; **20min**) where you have an opportunity to take a right turn (signposted 'DOLMEN') and make a short detour to visit the **Dolmen de Faldouët** burial chamber (**❷**; see Walk 11, page 52). Returning to the walk route, continue until you rejoin the B30 which you followed briefly at the start of the walk. Cross this main road to a continuation of the road you have been on. Then, after about 100 yards/metres, turn left at a T-junction. (A right turn here leads after some 150 yards/metres to a large undercover garden centre with an excellent restaurant serving snacks or full-scale meals.)

You are now on the the B28; after about ten minutes (**50min**) come to the car park at the northern entrance to the **Queen's Valley Reservoir** (**❸**). You have the option of walking along whichever side of the lake you prefer. I describe the path to your left, along the eastern side, but the path to the right on the western side is equally pleasant.

Within ten minutes come to a causeway; not far beyond

View from the path on the eastern shore of the lake (near Picnic 14)

it, there is a grassy area on the left (Picnic 14; photo above), where you can enjoy the view. Continue along the path, which now leads through a pleasant tree-lined stretch, eventually reaching the **dam** (**1h10min**) and overflow control tower at the southern end of the lake. This is just under a mile (1.5km) from the northern end of the reservoir.

Descend a steep winding path with steps and pass the water company's **pumping station** on your right, to reach a road, where you turn left. Ignore a turning that forks back to your left; keep straight along. After ten minutes the road bends sharply to the right and then, almost immediately, it heads left again. Now you'll again enjoy fine views of Mont Orgueil Castle in the distance. At **1h30min** come to La Rue Horman and turn right. Within a couple of minutes, you will see the sign for the **Jersey Pottery** (❹) on your left. There is no admission charge, and this pottery is well worth a visit at some point during your stay; like the garden centre already mentioned, it too has an excellent restaurant. There's also an art gallery offering exhibition space for local artists.

Reaching the end of the road at a T-junction, turn left into another road with a 'no entry' sign. This takes you to the main street of Gorey village. It's a pleasantly picturesque area with a few shops and a post office. Continue along the road; it takes you back to the lower end of the B30, not far from where the walk began. Turn right and go down the hill into **Gorey**, to your bus or car (⭕; **1h55min**).

Walk 15: LA HOUGUE BIE

See also photo on page 20
Distance: 3.5mi/5.5km; 1h15min
Grade: ● very easy
You will need: stout shoes
Access: 🚌 13 or 🚗 to La Hougue Bie (49° 12.104'N, 2° 3.867'W; free parking at ❶); return the same way
Short walk: La Hougue Bie — La Franche Ville — La Hougue Bie (2mi/4km; 55min; ● very easy; access as above). Follow the main walk to La Franche Ville (35min), then use the notes at the foot of page 61 to shorten the circuit back to La Hougue Bie.

I would usually apologise for suggesting a walk which stays predominantly on metalled roads, but in this case I won't. Not only do these lanes see little traffic, but they reveal a few Jersey peculiarities. And you wouldn't want to miss those, would you?

Start out at the fascinating site of **La Hougue Bie** (❶; Picnic 15). Its history goes back to Neolithic times, but became more colourful with the passage of the years. The centre of attention here is a high mound (40 feet/15 metres), excavated only during the 1900s, revealing a burial chamber — one of the ten oldest buildings in the world — which you can inspect by stooping along a narrow passage for some 50 feet/15 metres.

An old Jersey custom: 'marriage stones', built into the homes of newlyweds. They are to be found all over the island, but those illustrated below can be seen on the short version of this walk.

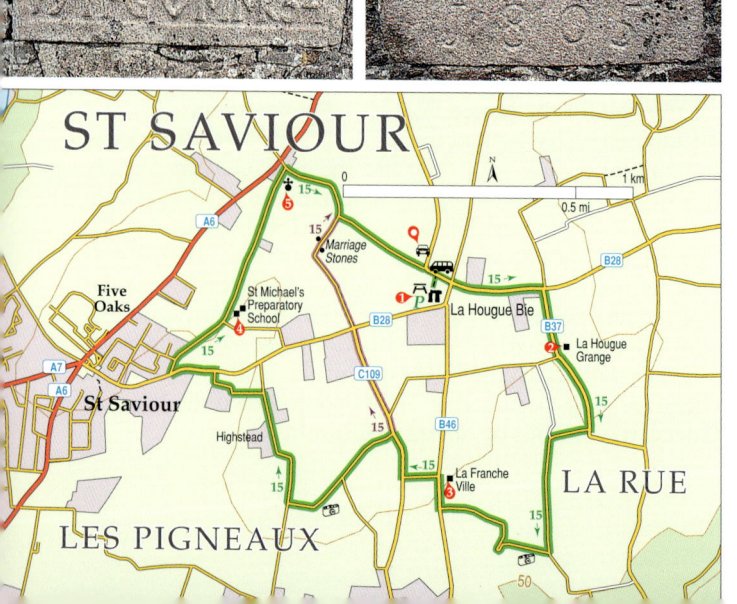

Walk 15: La Hougue Bie

On top of the mound are two chapels of 12th- and 16th-century origin. You can learn all about them in the information centre, which has a useful book section and modest refreshment facilities. There are also geological and archaeological exhibits here, as well as a memorial to occupation slave-workers housed in a wartime bunker which was once the German battalion command post for the eastern sector of the island.

Coming out of La Hougue Bie, turn right and then right again at the *second* crossroads (under **10min**). You pass the magnificent house and driveway of **La Hougue Grange** (❷), on your left. About 300 yards/metres futher on, look out for a lane on your right, just before the road makes a 90° turn to the left. Head along this lane, which turns left. Continue for ten minutes, until you can turn right on another lane. Along here you'll start getting magnificent views towards Grouville Bay. Drop down into a small valley and climb gently out of it. Come to a road and turn right, alongside **La Franche Ville** (❸), which has a fine granite wall worth seeing in its own right.

Where the wall ends, turn left on a short stretch of untarred road. Then turn right and quickly left (**35min**). *The Short walk keeps straight ahead here; see footnote below.**

Keep right where this lane forks, to gain a view over St Clement's Bay. Come to a T-junction and turn right, passing Highstead on the left. Turn left beyond it on Rue du Pré. After a quick succession of right, left and right turns, come to Prince's Tower Road. Turn left here and continue for 150 yards/metres, then go right into La Rue des Friquettes. You pass **St Michael's Preparatory School** (❹) on the right and soon see La Hougue Bie to the right.

At the next junction, come upon a **Methodist church** (❺) and turn right on a road. To see the **marriage stones** shown at the left (they are on the Short walk route), bear right for a few minutes at the next junction: the first is set beside a gate on your right; the second into a wall on your left. Then return to this road, pass La Commune (a three-storey house, noted as an early producer of Jersey cider), and regain **La Hougue Bie** (❶; **1h15min**).

*For the Short walk, keep ahead here, to a crossroads. Go straight over on a road which eventually descends gently and turns to the right. Now look out on your right for a wall into which is set the 'marriage stone' shown at the left. Further along, on your left, beside a gate, is the stone on the far left. Notice, too, the open brook beside the road: most brooks in Jersey are covered over, so that motorists don't bumble into them! Continue along the road to a right turn and head back past La Commune to La Hougue Bie.

BUSES AND INTER-ISLAND TRANSPORT

BUSES

LibertyBus, the official service (www.libertybus.je or telephone 01534 828555), is operated by Tower Transit UK under contract to, and in partnership with, the Government of Jersey. They offer a superb website, with 'Plan my journey', maps of all lines and all bus stops, and online real-time tracking. Moreover, when you are out and about, you can find out when the next bus is due by using your mobile: just send the bus stop number as a text to 66556 (each bus stop on the island has its individual number).

The buses themselves have a basic white livery, decorated with colourful 'sails'. Although a few bus stops are marked by signposts, most are indicated by markings on the road surface. Always wait at a bus stop: *drivers will not pick up passengers at intermediate points.* And *always flag down your bus*, even when waiting at a stop — every stop is considered a 'request' stop. For the same reason, always ring the bell when you want to alight from the bus.

At press date the basic adult ticket price is £2.70 for each journey; there are *many* 'hop on hop off' variations (see their website), but unless you plan to use the buses more than twice a day (to get to and from a walk), these offers may not be economical.

Because services are so numerous, it is not possible to print full timetables here. Instead, destinations are shown and the principal route number(s) serving them (note that where two or more services are shown, some will be weekdays only; some may be Sundays only). This listing includes not only the starting points for all the walks, but some of the island's tourist attractions. *A very approximate* frequency of services indicating the average time between buses is shown, but even so, there will be considerable variations. Note that services are often more frequent between 9am and mid-morning, and again from mid-afternoon until about 6pm. Note also: the details shown opposite are for **summer services** (1 June to 30 September). At other times of the year, be sure to obtain the winter timetable, which is often more restricted. *If you plan to make frequent use of the buses, do either call in at Liberation Station in St Helier or look online for timetables (and check if there are any faresaver tickets of interest).*

Where the service is so irregular that it is impossible to give an average timing, no frequency is given; *refer* to the timetables. Be aware that changes in service numbers and timings can take place at short notice.

Buses and inter-island transport

Destination	Route(s)	Approximate frequency	
		Weekdays	Sundays*
Airport	15, 22	20-30min	30-45min
Bonne Nuit Bay	4	1h	1h
Corbière, La	12, 12a, 22	45min-1h	1h-1h30
Devil's Hole	7	1h	none
'Durrell' (Jersey's zoo)	3, 13, 23	30-45min	30-45min
Etacq, L'	12a, 22	30-45min	1h
Gorey and the castle	1, 1a, 1g, 2	30min	30-45min
Green Island	1, 1g	30min	45min
Grève de Lecq, La	9	1h	1h
Grosnez (castle about a 10min walk)	8, 9	2h	none
Hamptonne Farm	7, 7a	1h	refer
Hougue Bie, La	13	30-45min	1h
Jersey Lavender	12, 12a, 15	45min-1h	1h-1h30
Jersey Pearl	22	30-45min	1h
Jersey Pottery, Gorey	1, 1a	30min	30-45min
Jersey War Tunnels	8, 28	45min-1h	45min-1h
Kempt Tower	22	30-45min	1h
Landes Racecourse, Les	8	2h	none
Mare Wine Estate, La	7, 28	1h	refer
Mielle de Morville, La	12a, 22	30-45min	1h
Old Portelet Inn	12a	1h30min	refer
Pallot Steam Museum (near)	5	1h30min	refer
Plémont	8	2h	none
Portelet Bay	12a	1h330min	refer
Queen's Valley Reservoir	13	30-45min	1h
Rozel Bay	3	1h	1h
St Aubin	12, 12a, 14, 15	10-15min	20-30min
St Brelade's Bay	12, 12a, 14	30min	30-45min
St Catherine's Bay	2, 2a	1h	refer
St John's Church	5, 7, 7a	1h-1h30min	refer
St Lawrence's Church	7, 7a	1h	refer
St Mary's Church	7	1h	1h
St Ouen's Bay	22	30-45min	1h
St Ouen's Parish Hall	8, 9	30-45min	30-45min
St Peter's Village	9	1h	refer
St Saviour's Hospital	13	30-45min	1h
Samares Manor	1a	30min	30-45min
Sorel (walk from St John's)	5, 7	1h-1h30min	refer
Tamba Park	7	1h	refer
Treasures of the Earth	22	30-45min	1h
Val de la Mare	9	30-45min	30-45min
Zoo ('Durrell')	3, 13 23	40min	1h *

On bank holidays, the Sunday bus service operates.

TRANSPORT TO OTHER ISLANDS (OR FRANCE)

Enquire at the Tourism Offices in St Helier for details of possible day excursions to Alderney, Guernsey, Sark or France.

Index

Geographical names comprise the only entries in this Index. For other entries, see Contents, page 3. A page number in *italic type* indicates a map; a page number in **bold type** indicates a photograph. Both of these may be in addition to a text reference on the same page. 'TM' refers to the walking map on the reverse of the touring map. See also bus timetable index on page 62.

Anne Port 11, 20, *47*
Archirondel 11, 19, *47*, 52
Beauport, Le 9, **11**, 14, 29, *30*
Belle Hougue, La 44, *TM*
Blanches Banques, Les *30*, 35
Bonne Nuit Bay 42, 44, 63, *TM*
Bouley Bay 11, 18, 44, 63, *TM*
Corbière, La 10, 14, 15, 29, *30*, **36**, 63, **cover**
Corbière Walk **5**, *30*, 35, **36, cover**
Coupe, La *47*, **49**
Couperon, Dolmen du *47*, 48, **48**
Croc, Le 21
Dannemarche Reservoir, Le 54
Devil's Hole **14**, 16, 17, 43, 63, *TM*
Douët de la Mer *47*, 48
'durrell' (see Jersey's zoo)
Elizabeth Castle 9, *25*, **28**
Etacq, L' 10, 14, 16, 40, 41, 63, *TM*
Faldouët, Dolmen de **20**, *47*, 52, 58
Flicquet *47*, 50, **51**
Gorey (Gouray) **12-13**, 20, 22, *47*, 58, 59, 63
 Bay and Pier *47*, **12-13**, 63
Grand Etacquerel, Le 10, 16, 40, 41, 63, *TM*
Green Island 63
Grève au Lanchon, La 43, *TM*
Grève de Lecq, La 16, 43, 63, *TM*
Grosnez (Gros Nez) 14, **16**, **40**, 42, 63,*TM*
Hamptonne Country Life Museum 53-5
Havre de Scez, Le 46, *47*, 48, **49**
Hocq, Le 21
Hougue Bie, La 11, 18, **20**, *60*, **60**, 63
Ile au Guerdain, L' **29**, *30*, 32, *33*
Jersey Lavender *TM*
Jersey War Tunnels (German Underground Military Hospital) 14, 17, *54*, *56*, **57**, 63
Jersey's zoo 18, **19**, 63, *TM*
Kempt Tower 11, 15, 38, 63
La Lande du Ouest 29, *30*
Landes, Les 41, 63, *TM*
Macpela Cemetery 18
Mare slipway, La 11, 46, *47*, 52
Marrioneux, Le 43, *TM*
Mielle de Morville, La 10, 16, 63
Mielles, Les **10**, 22, 35
Millbrook 14, 17; Millbrook Reservoir 53
Mont Orgueil 18, 20, *47*, **12-13**
 Castle *47*, **12-13**, 58

Monts Grantez, Dolmen des 39
Morel Farm 55
Moulin de Quetivel, Le 17, *56*
Nez, Le *54*-5
Noirmont 10, **15**, *30*, 32, *33*, **34**
North coast path 22, 40, 42-4, *TM*
Pallot Steam Museum **19**, 63
Petit Port, Le *30*, 36, 44, *TM*
Pinnacle, The 10, 40, **41**, *TM*
Plémont 16, 42, **43**, 63, *TM*
Portelet, Le 14, *30*, 32, *33*, 34
 Bay **29**, *30*, 32, *33*, 34, 63
 Common 14, 29, *30*, *33*
Ouaisné, L' 14, 29, *30*
Queen's Valley Reservoir 11, 21, *47*, 58, **59**, 63
Rocco Tower *30*, 35
Rocque, La **13**, 18, 21
Ronez 10, 17, *47*, *TM*
Rozel 11, 18, 19, 42, 44, 46, *47*, 49, 63, *TM*
 Bay *47*, 48, 63, *TM*
 Moulin de *47*, **48**
 Woods **2**, 11, **19**, 46, *47*, 49, *TM*
St Aubin 14, 22, *30*, 35, 63
St Brelade 9, 29, *30*
St Brelade's Bay 15, *30*, 63
St Catherine's Bay and Breakwater 18, 19, *47*, **51**, 52, 63
St Clement 21
St Helier 9, 14, 17, 18, *25*, **26-7**, 28, 62-3
 town plan *25*
St Lawrence 14, 17, 53, *54*, **55**, 63
 Millennium Standing Stone 53
St Martin's 46, *47*
St Mary's 14, 63
St Ouen's *37*, 39, 63
 Bay 10, 15, *30*, 35, **38**, 63
St Peter's Valley *56*, 57
St Saviour's Hospital 11, 20, *47*, 58, 63
Sergenté, La 15, *30*, 36
Sion 18
Sorel 43, **44**, 45, 63, *TM*
Tamba Park 17
Trinity 18, 63
Val de la Mare, Le 10, 16, *37*, **38**, 63
Vallée des Mouriers, La 43, 45, *TM*
Vaux Cuissin, Les *37*, 38, **39**
Waterworks Valley 11, 17, 53